GENESIS OF VANCOUVER (CITY)

EXPLORATIONS OF ITS SITE

1791, 1792 & 1808

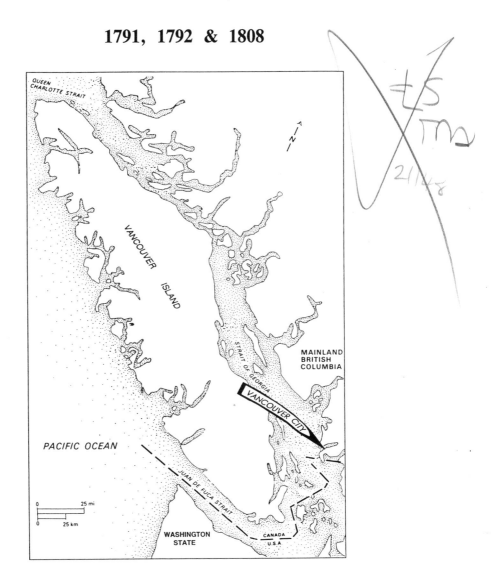

TOMAS BARTROLI

© 1997

Canadian Cataloguing in Publication Data

Bartroli, Tomas
      Genesis of Vancouver City
        Revised edition
      ISBN 0-9695250-2-8

DEDICATED TO
ANNE CARSON YANDLE
IN MEMORY OF PHILIP YANDLE

Printed by
Electric Print
1986 West 4th Ave.
Vancouver, B.C., Canada
V6J 1M5

Available from:
Marco Polo Books
3450 West 20th Ave.
Vancouver, B.C.
V6S 1E4
Fax: (604) 733-6484

CONTENTS

ACKNOWLEDGEMENTS

In preparing this book, I have received excellent suggestions and advice from the following persons: Professors Cole Harris and Alfred Siemens of the Geography Department, and Professor Emeritus John Norris, formerly of the History Department, all at the University of British Columbia; Lieutenant-Commander Andrew David, formerly attached to the Hydrographic Office of the British Ministry of Defence, in Taunton, England; Mr. Gary Penway of the Corporation of the District of North Vancouver; and Mr. R.C. Harris, a civil engineer, very interested in Northwest history. I have also received very efficient assistance from archives and libraries in Spain, Mexico, the United States of America, and England, and from the library of the University of British Columbia, Canada. Mr. Nicholas Doe, also an engineer interested in Northwest history, contributed data and many comments, edited drafts, and provided the index.

The aforementioned Hydrographic Office, the Naval Museum in Madrid, Spain, and the Mexican National Archives, have authorized me to publish passages from manuscripts and copies of charts and drawings they hold.

I am most grateful to these persons and institutions, and to others, for contributing, in different ways, to the production of this book.

Chapter 1

INTRODUCTION

Along a coastline bounded by the steep rocky slopes of the Coast Mountains, the Fraser Delta is unique. Over geological time, glaciers and the Fraser River, which drains over a quarter of the province of British Columbia, have filled with sediments, in places several kilometres thick, a valley which at its widest stretches from Point Atkinson in West Vancouver, ninety kilometres south to Bellingham in the United States. For many thousands of years, the southern part of this delta front has been inactive, fed only by the Nooksack River, and so circumstances determined that the city of Vancouver would arise north of the border in Canada where the combination of the river estuary, the deep-water harbour of Burrard Inlet, and access to the passes eastward through the Rocky Mountains to the prairies beyond, afforded all that was needed for the development of a great port.

The site of the present city of Vancouver was probably first occupied by Native people shortly after the end of the last ice age, some ten thousand years ago.

Yet, not until the first European seafarers reached the outer coast in the 1770s was their long, but almost completely unrecorded history linked to that of the rest of the world.

Even after the first contact between the Native people and the outsiders from Europe, America, and the Orient, the transformation from a landscape of great forests and occasional grasslands to the urban area of today proceeded at a leisurely pace. The small fur-trading and farming post at Langley was not established until 1827. The gold-rush days of the 1850s and 1860s, and the rapid decline in the Native population, spurred on the growth of the immigrant settlement at New Westminster, the one-time capital of the province, but not until April 6, 1886, following the announcement that the then logging camp of

Granville would be the western terminal of the Canadian Pacific Railway did Vancouver start on its way to becoming the metropolis it is today.

The purpose of this book is to explore the genesis of this great city; that fleeting moment in history between the arrival of the first exploratory expeditions of the Europeans and the beginning of immigrant settlement in the Fraser Valley in the 1820s. The area to be considered approximates fairly closely to that of the present Greater Vancouver Regional District which is bounded in the south by the 49th parallel marking the border with the United States, in the north by the North Shore Mountains about forty-five kilometres from the border, in the east by the central Fraser Valley about fifty-five kilometres from the sea, and in the west by the Strait of Georgia. Vancouver itself is situated close to the estuary of the Fraser River on the northern side of the Fraser Valley at the point where the valley reaches the sea at latitude $49°15'$N, longitude $123°07'$W; however, within the Greater Vancouver area lie ten other cities,[1] some older than Vancouver, and several districts and towns[2] with a combined population that in the 1990s is rapidly approaching two million.

From time immemorial the Native people, or "Indians" as they were initially mistakenly called, had dwelt in villages and camps, and nourished themselves from the natural products of the sea, river, and land. But toward the end of the eighteenth century, geographical and historical circumstances made it inevitable that the site would be "discovered" by men of the two European empires that were colonizing North America, namely, Spain and Great Britain. Spain had established itself in what is now Mexico, but laid claim, in the imperialistic fashion of the time, to all of the North American continent roughly south and west of a line from New Orleans at the mouth of the Mississippi to Alaska. Largely as a result of the Russian "incursions" into Alaska beginning with the voyage of Bering and Chirikov in 1741, Spain had established a naval base at San Blas in Mexico in 1768 and was anxious to assert its claimed authority along the whole of the Pacific coast. Great Britain had dominion over the

---

[1] New Westminster (1860), Richmond (1879), Surrey (1879), Coquitlam (1891), Burnaby (1892), North Vancouver City (1907), Port Coquitlam (1913), Port Moody (1913), Langley City (1955), and White Rock (1957).

[2] Langley Township (1873), Maple Ridge (1874), Delta (1879), North Vancouver District (1892), West Vancouver (1912), and Pitt Meadows (1914).

northern and eastern side of the continent, having gained control by the Peace of Paris in 1763 of all of the French possessions, including Louisiana east of the Mississippi. Canadian fur traders, led by the Scotsman Alexander Mackenzie, were the first to reach the Pacific coast overland from the east in 1793, and the British were intensely interested in the possibility of a navigable passage between the North Pacific and Atlantic Oceans. Great Britain did not recognize Spain's claims to unvisited and unsettled areas north of the missions that Spain had established in California; a disagreement that almost led to a war between them in the 1790s.

Both empires sent naval expeditions to chart the coast between California and the Alaskan Peninsula, which was at the time still unknown to the world at large. Spain's first expedition was in 1774 (Pérez). Other voyages were made in 1775 (Hezeta and Bodega Quadra) and 1779 (Arteaga and Bodega Quadra), and continued with increasing frequency after 1788. The first exploration on behalf of Great Britain was effected by James Cook in 1778. Following Cook's voyage, fur traders of British, and shortly after American, nationality visited the coast to trade with the Native people for pelts of sea otter and other animals which were taken to the port of Canton for sale. In the process, the fur traders "discovered" and charted parts of the coast, particular those that offered a sheltered anchorage.

The early explorations failed to reveal the existence of the Juan de Fuca Strait, but this was redressed in July 1787 by the British fur-trader Charles Barkley (or Barclay) and his wife who chanced upon its twenty-kilometre wide entrance while sailing southward along the outer coast of Vancouver Island from Clayoquot Sound. During the subsequent two years, British and Spanish navigators entered the strait without revealing much more of its nature until, in 1790, a Spanish explorer (Quimper) penetrated to its eastern end, where navigable water lanes were observed through the San Juan Islands. These subsequently, in 1791 (Eliza), proved to provide access to what is now called the Strait of Georgia.

The stretch of coastline between Boundary Bay and the Burrard Inlet, was explored partially by the Spanish expedition of 1791, notably during an excursion into the Strait of Georgia led by José María Narváez. However, it was left to two bigger and much-better equipped expeditions of 1792 to complete the details, particularly of the inside of Burrard Inlet: a Spanish naval expedition of 1792 led by Dionisio Alcalá Galiano; and a British naval expedition by George Vancouver who was eventually to give his name to the city. Both of these expeditions made contact with the local inhabitants, and the records of their surveys, together with brief notes from the Spanish expedition of the previous year, contain the first written descriptions we have of the area and its pre-contact inhabitants.

These coastal explorations, along with others mentioned in the following pages, made it possible for the first time to produce charts of the Pacific Northwest in which the coastline is depicted with considerable accuracy. The earliest of such charts was one published in Spain in 1795; others appeared in England from about 1798 onwards. But although these late-eighteenth century charts showed, correctly enough, the lower part of the Columbia River between the present states of Washington and Oregon, nothing was shown of the Fraser River. This had to wait another fifteen or so years, until in 1808, a party of *voyageurs* and Native Americans, led by the Scotsman Simon Fraser with two fur-trader colleagues, explored most of the river that now bears his name.

Even then, it was not Fraser himself who produced a map of the river; this was left to his friend David Thompson who was in the process of gathering data on what he called "the northwest territory of the Province of Canada." Thompson's map, which incorporated all of Fraser's work, was drawn in 1813–1814, and included the courses of both the Fraser and Columbia Rivers. It gave the location of mountains and other geographic features, and was accompanied by some informative, but all-too brief notes. This was the earliest cartographic work in which was shown the Greater Vancouver area, including the north arm of its river, with an indication that it might be safely accessible from the Pacific Ocean by vessels of moderate size.

Thompson's map, which was produced for the North West Company, created great interest among the fur-trading community, and this was eventually to be followed-up by an employee of the Hudson's Bay Company which inherited the Columbia district from the North West Company in the merger of 1821. This employee, yet another Scotsman, James McMillan, again in the company of French-Canadians, *métis*, and Native people, followed the course of the Nicomekl River from Boundary Bay, portaged to the Fraser River, and reached what is now Mission in 1824.[3] He returned to the ocean by way of the south (main) arm of the Fraser River. It was this reconnaissance of the Fraser Valley

---

[3] The group also included several Hawaiians (Kanakas), an Englishman, and an American. The journal of one of the expedition clerks, John Work, who was of Irish descent, has survived.

that led directly to the establishment of Fort Langley, the first European settlement in the Greater Vancouver area.

This book analyzes the explorations of Narváez (1791), Vancouver (1792), Galiano (1792), and Fraser (1808) on the basis of all of the existing data. This data provides only a few details about the geographical realities of the Vancouver area at that point in time, and there is no firm documentary basis for a description of what might have been those realities; nevertheless, in the following pages it is possible to form what might be called "learned-guesses" on the subject, and I include such a description in Chapter 2.

*****

The European explorations of 1791, 1792, and 1808, constitute the gestation, the prelude, the genesis, of Vancouver and its surrounding cities. A fairly specific title for this book might have been, "The earliest recorded explorations of the site of Vancouver City, from the sea and from land"; however, for the sake of using a short title, I dared settle for *Genesis of Vancouver City*.

DATA

The still-existing data on these explorations is scant, and also confusing in several respects, particularly concerning the explorations effected by José Maria Narváez and by Simon Fraser. In the case of Narváez, all that is available are a few comments in reports from his fellow expeditionary members, and the chart and sketches in which the area of interest is depicted, very inaccurately, presumably on the basis of a sketch drawn by Narváez himself. In the case of Fraser, the surviving documents he wrote describing his exploration are very informative and interesting, but do not contain much detail. The part that is of the most immediate interest is, in my opinion, confusing as a result of his brevity.

On different occasions, up to the time of completing this text, I did my best to discover additional firsthand information, be it from Narváez,[4] from Fraser,

---

[4] Narváez spent the last years of his life in the Mexican city of Guadalajara, where he died in 1840. There are reliable indications that he possessed some written records and charts concerning his voyages to the Northwest Coast, and that these were kept by his relatives for some years after his death. These have now been lost.

or from other reliable contemporary sources. But after extensive searches, I have found none, and conclude that there probably is none.

Much of the essential data appears in four books edited, and where necessary translated, by Wagner, Lamb, and Kendrick. These are listed in the Bibliography section and are frequently referred to in this work. Because these books contain extensive indexes, I have not specified the page numbers in references to them, as they may be found easily enough without. However, concerning the Galiano expedition, this book includes details culled from unpublished documents.

Altogether, the existing data is not really detailed enough to provide a clear and thorough picture of the explorers' experiences and findings. Certainly, by skipping difficulties, omitting details, dramatising some events, and adding fictional padding, exciting accounts of these four explorations can be, and have been, composed. I firmly disapprove of such procedures, but approve of using comments and even, provided that such use is made quite clear to the reader, of providing suppositions, or possible scenarios regarding points, matters, events on which the existing data is not informative enough. I do so in this work.

Having studied all the data, I affirm that a number of publications that deal with the subject matter in some aspect or other, have assertions that contradict the data. As a contribution to setting straight the historic record, I offer this book hoping that it has few inaccuracies or flaws.

SPELLING

In this book, the spelling of the names of people and places sometimes differs from that commonly used today. These spellings, especially those that occur in quotations, are in keeping with the spelling of the original text. Some names are written in more than one way; for instance, *Florida Blanca* or *Floridablanca*, and *Zepeda* or *Cepeda*. Nowadays, the surnames Valdés and López require the sign for stress, and such stress marks are used in this book except when mentioning the names of islands, Valdes Island for example, which are written as they appear on current Canadian maps and charts. Dionisio Alcalá Galiano are the first and two surnames of an officer who is occasionally referred to as Galiano in some Spanish documents and also in this work. There are explanations for these and other linguistic oddities in this text, and the reader should not assume errors or misprints, unless proved by checking the records. Present-day toponyms are written as in current official gazetteers, except when specified otherwise in the text.

The spelling of names of places in Native languages (mostly of the Coast Salish family in this work) presents some difficulty in that the spelling is merely an attempted phonetic rendering of the Native pronunciation, which itself varies according to dialect. Over the years, considerable variation in the spelling has occurred, and no doubt a certain amount of inaccuracy. Spelling these names according to the International Phonetic Alphabet would create some practical difficulties, and accordingly I have opted, rightly or wrongly, to use the spelling most often encountered in historical papers published in English in the twentieth-century, with, where they exist, more up-to-date variations in parentheses the first time they occur in the text. Several Native toponyms, for example Coquitlam and Chilliwack, have entered mainstream Canadian usage and are written just as any other present-day toponym.

Chapter 2

THE SITE AND ITS INHABITANTS CIRCA 1790

Published studies provide a fairly reliable basis for conclusions to be drawn about the physical geography of the Greater Vancouver area circa 1790, but about the people that were here, and their way of life at that time, less is easily discerned. Yet, some notions may be formed from archaeological, historical, and ethnological studies, and from collections of the accounts and stories of the Native people themselves.

THE SITE

The coast has two dominating landmarks: a small peninsula called Point Roberts which is particularly conspicuous when seen from the south; and a rounded bluff forming the western termination of a wooded promontory at Point Grey. From Point Roberts, north to Point Grey, the coast is low, featureless, and barely discernible from the Strait of Georgia. Between Point Grey and Point Atkinson is the entrance to the Burrard Inlet, which is the southernmost inlet of the Coast Mountains. It was much the same in 1790. There have been some minor changes, particularly around the area of Lost Lagoon in Stanley Park and False Creek. Where in the park there is now a freshwater lake and a neck of dry land, was in the past only a slight obstacle to the portage of canoes from the inner part of Burrard Inlet to English Bay, and the land there may even have been regularly inundated during exceptionally high tides. The silhouette of the hill that dominates Stanley Park, when seen from the sea at a distance, must have seemed then to be a small island. False Creek has been extensively filled and reduced in area in modern times. There were many creeks along the shores of Point Grey, English Bay, and around Burrard Inlet, many of them flowing year-round. Perhaps the shoals called Roberts Bank and Sturgeon Bank that fringe the shoreline between Point Grey and Point Roberts were more extensive than today; certainly the river dropped a far greater quantity of driftwood and other vegetation.

The river and its delta dominated the region. All low riparian land was seasonally flooded. During the extraordinary flood of 1892, the river level rose over seven metres in some parts of the Lower Mainland, and in 1894 it rose so high that steamers floated on the streets of Chilliwack.[5] On the river and in Burrard Inlet, travelling by canoe was usually easy enough provided allowance was made for the tides and current. Sea canoeing between Point Roberts and Point Grey was hazardous in bad weather, as it remains so today for small craft.

The river was a huge source of food, among the largest of such on the North American continent. As well as runs of different species of salmon, there were large seasonal catches to be had of oolichan (eulachon), smelt, herring, sturgeon, and many other fishes. Seals frequented the lower river, and there were many whales in the Strait of Georgia. Rich beds of clams and mussels were found at many points along the coast, crabs were plentiful, and on the river and in the estuary there were huge flocks of waterfowl. The land yielded less food, but there were deer, elk, bears, lynx, cougars, wolves, and raccoons in the lower forests, and goats in the mountains to the north. Herds of elk roamed in Point Grey and around False Creek. This was a region of great natural abundance.

Above the floodline, and away from the bogs, some quite extensive, was a massive coniferous forest dominated by red cedar, Douglas fir, and, to a lesser extent, hemlock. Under the canopy of this huge forest, in which the largest trees were over a hundred metres tall, the forest floor was often quite open; where light penetrated there was likely to be a tangle of shrubs and deciduous trees that humans could hardly penetrate.

Regimes of precipitation and temperature were approximately what they are now, except that winters were longer and colder. Glaciers in the mountains to the north were much larger than today, and during many winters the Fraser River itself was frozen for a few weeks at a time.

---

[5] A report of "Explorations of New Westminster District" by John Fannin in 1873, says, "the Pitt River contains an area of nearly 20,000 acres, which is subject to overflow from all sides. The whole plain is nearly surrounded by water, so that diking is, in my opinion, out of the question." From the booklet *British Columbia Information for Emigrants*, published in London in 1873 and reprinted in 1875.

THE INHABITANTS

The population of this area in 1790 cannot be established with any reliability. An epidemic of smallpox had devastated the region in the early 1780s, leaving the survivors vulnerable to attacks from northern Vancouver Island where people had not been so badly affected by the disease. Quite possibly, the population in 1790 in what is now Greater Vancouver was not more than a tenth of what it had been a decade before. Perhaps only a thousand people wintered in this rich, depopulated region, but we do not know that for sure.

The following winter villages appear to have been occupied circa 1790, their populations far smaller and their number probably far fewer than a decade before: the Kwantlen (*Qw'ontl'en*) villages on the north bank of the Fraser just above New Westminster; two villages at Musqueam near the mouth of the north arm of the Fraser; and Tsawwassen on the coast between Point Roberts and the mouth of the south arm of the Fraser. Perhaps there were winter villages (but some or all of these may have been spring or summer villages) at *Stselax* (*Stsulawh*), near Musqueam; at *Eyalmu* (*Ee'yullmough*) behind Jericho Beach; at *Snauq* (*Sun'ahk*) on the southwest side of Burrard Bridge; and at *Whoi-Whoi* (*Khwaykhway*) on the site of Lumberman's Arch in Stanley Park. There were probably seasonal Cowichan and Nanaimo fishing villages on Lulu Island or a little further upriver. The Squamish probably migrated seasonally into Burrard Inlet, where some of them may have wintered.

People lived in winter villages from late November to March, dependent largely on food obtained at other times, where they engaged in a round of ceremonial activities. In March, they moved out in small groups to local resource-procurement sites, and in summer many of them went upriver to the foot of the Fraser Canyon, just beyond Yale, to catch and dry salmon. In late fall, a large number collected at the mouth of the Pitt River to socialize and gather Indian potato (wapato). Such was the broad outline of intricate fishing, gathering, and hunting economies that depended on detailed local knowledge, skills acquired over centuries and handed down through the generations, and the use of a great variety of plants and animals.

Social life revolved primarily around the house group, most of whose members were relatives, and intricate webs of kin relations that bound people in different villages together. The village itself was a weak social unit, and although the heads of different house groups met frequently over the winter months, no one had much coercive authority outside his or her own house group. Resource-procurement sites were owned by house groups, not by villages. This was a diffuse, decentred social system that, as they entered the region, Europeans, accustomed to much more explicit social hierarchies, failed to understand.

The peoples of the region warred at various times with most of their neighbours. Theirs was a rich resource that only alliances, force, or the threat of force could protect. In many places around the Strait of Georgia, and probably in the Greater Vancouver area too, people defended themselves with forts and watchtowers. There is some general evidence that the scale and intensity of warfare increased as firearms were introduced; however, essentially, the history of warfare in the region is unknown.

Here, as elsewhere in North America, every detail of the life of the Aboriginal people was infused with spirit power. Spirit power was readily transferred between individuals, animals, plants, rocks, and weather; the distinctions, so habitually made by the European mind, between people and nature, the animate and inanimate, the observer and the observed, were not made by the Natives. They lived with benevolent and malevolent spirits that could be invoked or propitiated in various ways, and whose power was pervasive. Few of the particular regional details of this cosmology are known, much less than for the Katzie, the people who lived a little farther upriver, along the Pitt.

Overall, perhaps the singular most-important fact about the region in 1790 is that it had been recently, massively depopulated, and that the survivors were trying to pick up the pieces after the great demographic disaster that had befallen them.

*****

In the following paragraphs I give some summaries of common assumptions regarding the Native people and their way of life.

They did NOT have: cereals, citrus fruits, salt; poultry, cows, bulls, horses, donkeys; ceramics, earthenware articles; or efficient metal tools. Nor did they build tall totems and funeral structures of the kind made in more northern parts of the Northwest Coast. Nor did they use sails on their canoes; and they had no kayaks. None of their buildings were made of stone.

They did make use of: edible vegetables: roots, camas, Indian potatoes, a sort of garlic or onion, berries of different varieties; fur and leather from sea otter, beaver, wolf, bear; wood, especially red cedar; sinews, fibres, and seaweed.

Perhaps they had: domestic dogs; native copper, found randomly in the soil; bits and pieces of iron obtained from intertribal trade, or found in pieces of driftwood.

They did NOT practice: agriculture; whaling, as did the Nuu-chah-nulth and other peoples of the outer coast; nor is there any hint that they made human sacrifices.

Activities they pursued included: canoeing, fishing, digging for shellfish; hunting and trapping birds, wildfowl, and wild animals; fruit and berry picking, wild vegetable harvesting (mostly by women); gathering and working wood; dressing hides; house building; and local and extra-local trade.

Products: All that was needed was made from wood, wood fibres, bone, grease, shells, gum, grasses, etc.

They manufactured: baskets, rakes, pikes, boxes, bowls, rattles, spoons, rope; woven-textured articles such as: garments, mats, blankets, hats; waterproof containers; tools: adzes, knives, tongs; weapons: clubs, spears, bows and arrows, helmets, coats of armour (made mostly with leather); canoes made from thick cedar logs hollowed out by burning the log core, with seats installed, perhaps with some decoration or symbol; paddles; and ornaments made from cold-hammered native copper ore.

Habitation: They lived near sources of potable water, mostly on the waterfront. Many communities moved from site to site during the year so as to make the most of the hunting and fishing seasons. In many cases there was a sizeable main village in a sheltered location, used mostly in wintertime. Temporary or seasonal camps were made at fishing sites. Villages were generally rows of houses, most houses being large enough to be shared by two or more families. Residences at seasonal camps may have been simple wooden shacks. In some places, Musqueam for example, villages were fortified with a ditch and walls of planks. All dwellings had nearby canoe-launching sites.

Family or communal houses: The most-used building material was red cedar. The frame was a rectangle of upright posts sunk into the ground. Thinner logs were laid, horizontally, on top of these posts, connecting them together. Overlapping boards were laid on these logs, forming a rectangular slanted roof so rain water would run off and drop to the ground outside the building. Heavy rocks were placed on parts of the roof, to keep boards in

13

position. Side walls were thin boards held to the vertical posts by rope or reeds. Doorways were small to prevent ingress by bears.

House interiors had: low platforms of earth or wood, along the walls; hanging curtains or mats arranged to divide the platforms into small sections, one for each family. The middle of the floor was empty, except for one or more fireplaces made with a circle of rocks. Roof boards could be moved sideways for making an opening for smoke to emerge. These were manoeuvred by a person standing on the ground and using a long pole; likewise for re-setting roofing. Boxes of different sizes were used for storing goods; large boxes were laid on platforms, against the walls. Reserves of dry or smoked fish were hung from stringers laid across the rafters.

Outside the homes: were racks for drying fish; garbage heaps; and spots for keeping canoes.

Procedure for changing dwelling sites: Leaving the vertical house posts in position, boards of roofing and siding were removed and laid on two canoes, side-by-side, catamaran style. Household belongings were placed on the boards and with skilful navigation the whole load was transported to another site for assemble into another home. Frequently-used alternative sites would have had permanently-standing vertical posts. Perhaps a few persons were left on the site of a winter village while the rest of the villagers were away.

Food: The enormous abundance of non-agricultural food probably determined their diet: fish and shellfish was the basis together with some meat and a small proportion of easily obtainable vegetables: herbs, roots, camas bulbs, wild onions. Berries: salal, huckleberries, salmonberries, thimbleberries, gooseberries, strawberries. Fruit: crabapples, plums, rosehips. Fish was cured in summertime for consumption in winter.

Cooking methods included: roasting over the fire and stewing. The technique was to build a good fire, and have nearby a supply of rocks and a watertight bowl or box containing water and chunks of fish or meat. Rocks were placed on the fire. Using wooden tongs, the hot rocks were picked up and dropped into the cooking vessel until the food was stewed.

Beverages would have been: water, cold or warm, perhaps occasionally sweetened with berry juice.

Clothing: They wore simple garments, some made only of fibre, others with fibre and fur trimming; cloaks made of fur. The favourite kind was sea otter worn mainly by chiefs, and mostly for ceremonial purposes. Men generally wore one garment only, perhaps none at all when weather was hot. Women generally wore at least a garment around the waist, and often a short cape (tippet) covering the shoulder and chest. People usually went about barefoot, but in cold or rainy weather they might have wrapped their feet. They wore waterproof hats of braided fibre with tops of conical shape. Chiefs' hats were more elaborate than those of commoners (see hat in the Chief's portrait reproduced in Plate 20.)

Personal ornamentation: included cosmetics made with grease, sometimes red ochre, crushed mica, and soot. They drew lines and shapes on their faces, and the men also on their chests. They dressed their hair, wore necklaces and bracelets. Women did NOT wear a labret (a small solid disk inset in the inner part of the lower lip, causing it to protrude) as was the case in communities of more northern parts.

Art: Artistic interest and ability was expressed in form, shape, and colour. Carving and painting of boxes, masks, house posts, etc. was popular. Art was produced for aesthetic pleasure, but perhaps also with some social or spiritual connotation, as a symbolic representation of spiritual power, aiming to influence the future, to enhance significance of events, or to commemorate the dead.

Social structure, mores: The family was the social basis. Society was strongly conditioned by notions of wealth, rank, prestige, and family bonds. There were standard formal codes of behaviour and ethics; a social strata ranging from chiefs to slaves; village chiefs, mostly males with special privileges including being allowed to have more than one wife. Heredity was the basis for chieftainship. Perhaps there were shamans, again mostly men, considered to have spiritual and medical powers to cure bodily ailments, communicate with spirits, provide spells, foretell the future. Women were generally subservient to men, occupied in cooking, vegetable picking, spinning, and weaving. Adulterers were punished or ostracised. They kept slaves of both sexes, who were mostly obtained from raids on rival communities, and who were compelled to do menial tasks. Probably there was a loose aggregation of villages bound by territorial and linguistic unity, perhaps alliances of some tribes, perhaps a common leader in case of raids or warfare; however, perhaps no centralized organization, no hereditary overlord with recognized authority over large number of communities, or over an extensive territory.

Social contacts, entertainment: There were alliances between families or bands strengthened by intermarriages. Individuals or groups visited others to barter. Complex arrangements were made between one band and another for weddings. Special rites were performed at puberty for girls. Intertribal visits were occasions for story-telling, theatrical performances, singing, drum-beating, hand-clapping, dancing, games; athletic competitions: canoeing, wrestling, etc. Wintertime festivals were mostly held indoors. Feasts were convoked by families or bands and aimed to maintain status and confirm claims to certain spots, and even to exclusive use of certain symbols, songs, and personal names.

Potlatches: were gatherings marking corporate events and held on a village or household level. They required prior accumulation of wealth in terms of food, goods, and objects and were convoked mostly by chiefs. Motivations for potlatches were redistribution of wealth; insurance; solemnization of the transfer of chiefly rights; celebration of major points in the annual life cycle; cementing political and family ties; and demonstrations of pride and perhaps some boastfulness. Invitations were sent out to chiefs, families, and bands. There was a ceremonial welcome to guests, lavish meals, presents, and entertainment. Leading guests would subsequently respond in similar manner.

Tribal rivalries: There were occasional mobilizations of men with weapons, for raids or warfare, and intertribal skirmishes. Only men participated. The victors sometimes plundered and appropriated persons, particularly women and children, as slaves or hostages. The motivations for violence included retaliation, greed, natural resource control, and punishment for alleged offence.

Religion: As do people the world over, they told stories and myths about the origins of mankind. They performed ceremonies and indulged in other practices to invoke goodwill or help from forces, powers, assumed to have influence on mankind, nature, the weather. There were rites and practices for cleansing and purification which could include sexual abstention, self-flagellation, and temporary isolation. There were funeral and burial rites and they had cemeteries, and special burial places for chiefs.

*****

To repeat, this is only a tentative description of what <u>may</u> have been the facts about the site studied here, and its inhabitants, around 1790.

Chapter 3

NORTH AMERICA BETWEEN 1773 AND 1790

Between 1773 and 1790, Russia, Spain, and Great Britain, then major world powers, were active on the Northwest Coast of North America.

Russian traders were obtaining furs from the Native hunters of the islands and mainland of the northwesternmost part of the coast now belonging to the United States' state of Alaska. Thus far, Russia had no presence south of the 60th parallel, but there were reports and rumours of its intention to establish outposts and settlements further south.

Spain held dominion over large parts of both North and South America through its viceroyalties of New Spain (Mexico City), New Granada (Bogotá), Peru (Lima), and La Plata (Buenos Aires). On its Pacific coast, New Spain, now Mexico and Central America, had an important naval base at Acapulco, and smaller ones at San Blas, San Diego, and Monterey. With arguments that carried no weight internationally, the Spanish rulers had long claimed, and continued to claim, that Spain had exclusive sovereignty over American territories further north. Alarmed by rumours of Russian intentions to expand their activities, Spain began, in 1774, to explore the Pacific coast, north of the present-day (upper) California.

BRITISH DOMAIN - FUR TRADE

For several centuries prior to 1776, Great Britain, and until shortly before, France, had held dominion over much of the northeast of North America. Their domain included the thirteen colonies on the Atlantic coast, which, during that year, gained independence and formed the original United States of America.

Subsequently, Great Britain retained the territory of what was then a fledging Canada, territory that is now part of the provinces of Quebec and Ontario.

As a seafaring nation, Great Britain had a long-standing interest in finding a navigable passage between the Atlantic and the Pacific Oceans at high latitudes, what in Western Europe was called "the Northwest Passage." The British government supported and encouraged exploration aimed at locating such a passage, whether by ships examining the northern shores of the continent, or by parties traversing the land by way of the lakes and rivers of the interior.

Much of the country that now constitutes the central Canadian provinces was sparsely populated at the time. In this vast area, British companies were engaging in two activities that in some respects were interrelated: trade and geographic exploration.

The principal trade was in furs: beaver, muskrat, otter, fox, lynx, etc. It was carried out by groups that typically included people of varying descent: British with a high proportion of Scots, French, *métis*, and Native Americans who acted as guides. Initially, many such groups acted as independent traders, the *coureurs de bois*, but later they joined commercial companies that exported a variety of goods, mainly furs, to Europe and thence imported manufactured ones in return.

The largest company engaged in the fur trade was the Hudson's Bay Company, chartered in 1670, with headquarters in London, England, and with prerogatives and obligations regulated more or less effectively by the British government. It had a base at Fort Churchill. Other smaller forts and outposts were scattered throughout the region drained by the various rivers that flow into Hudson Bay, but with its own trading territory fairly secure, it was for many years not very active in expanding its domain.

Besides the Hudson's Bay Company, there were many small companies of traders and *voyageurs* which eventually coalesced to form a large conglomerate known as the North West Company with its headquarters in Montréal. Thence the traders, with the essential help of the Native Americans, made their way along the St. Lawrence River and contiguous waterways, and portaged between waterways to reach Lake Superior, Lake Winnipeg, and beyond into the extensive system of lakes and rivers that drain into the Arctic Ocean in what is now northern Saskatchewan. The smaller companies and its voyageurs increasingly operated in territories farther west than those of the Hudson's Bay Company, and as the lines of communication between these western outposts and central Canada grew longer and longer, there was an increasing interest in finding easier, cheaper ways of reaching the sea by way of what is now the provinces of Alberta and British Columbia. For a people that travelled whenever they could by canoe, as did the Native people, the most sought-after routes were of course interconnected lakes and rivers.

For their trading posts and supply bases, the fur traders established, at convenient places, what they called forts. These generally consisted of one or more simple buildings within a wooden stockade protected with firearms, to which the local hunters would bring their pelts to barter for imported goods.

In this manner, the fur-trading companies advanced westward across the country, and sometime, probably in the early 1750s, came within sight of the Rocky Mountains. At the time there was little appreciation of the distance, or of the difficulty of the terrain that lay beyond, the land that is now British Columbia. The Rocky Mountains are but the easternmost range of the Cordilleran region of Canada, which consists of four mountain chains parallel to one another, with a total width of about 650 kilometres. Its largest range, the Rocky Mountains, with snow-capped peaks of high altitude, is the continental divide where rivers run in different directions; some go north to the Arctic Ocean, some east to the Atlantic Ocean, and some, such as the Fraser and the Columbia, run westward to the Pacific Ocean. The fur-trading companies aimed to cross the Cordilleran region and make their way to the shores of the Pacific Ocean; and by 1788 they were making good, but inevitably slow progress in this endeavour.

Events on the mainland between 1770 and 1788

- *1771-2* — Samuel Hearne, of the Hudson's Bay Company, setting out from Fort Churchill, on the shores of Hudson Bay, follows and reconnoitres the Coppermine River all the way to the Arctic Ocean.
- *1774* — Hudson's Bay Company builds Cumberland House on the Saskatchewan River.
- *1778* — Peter Pond, an American trader, establishes an outpost in the territory of present-day Alberta.
- *1779* — Nine independent trading concerns pool efforts on a temporary basis.
- *1783-4* — Those partnerships coalesce, forming a major fur-trading company known as the North West Company. Its members (called "Nor'Westers") include Peter Pond, Alexander Mackenzie, and Simon Fraser.

- *1786* — Aiming to reach the Pacific Ocean, but terminating in the Arctic, Alexander Mackenzie reconnoitres the river that bears his name.
- *1788* — The North West Company builds Fort Chipewyan, near Athabaska Lake in present-day Alberta.

THE NORTHWEST COAST OF AMERICA

Juan de Fuca Strait

Although prior to 1774, Russia had been active on the northernmost parts of the Pacific coast of the American continent, the coast between latitudes 43°N and 56°N remained unvisited by foreigners. It was outside the realm of European public knowledge. Yet, in spite of this, maps and texts were published in Europe showing imagined coastlines, straits, and other features. The basis for these conjectural geographical features were reports that mariners in the service of Spain had, in earlier centuries, discovered on at least two occasions, navigable passages across the top of the North American continent.

One such account (divulged for the first time in a book written by Michael Lok and published in England in 1625) made the following, summarized assertions:

> In the year 1592, a voyage of that kind was carried out by a man (a Greek), whose real name was Apostolos Valerianos, who was serving in the Spanish Navy, in which he was known by the name of Juan de Fuca. Commanding an expedition with two vessels, he set out from the Mexican port of Acapulco, on the American Pacific coast. He sailed northward, and, on the part of that coast situated between the 47th and the 48th degrees of latitude, he discovered a broad inlet; he navigated through it, and along contiguous water lanes that ran between lands "rich in gold, silver, and pearls," and inhabited by people clad in furs. Eventually his expedition reached "the North Sea," whence he returned to Acapulco.

This text, written in English, and unaccompanied by any chart, subsequently formed the only established basis for the story of Juan de Fuca. It implied that he had discovered, for Spain, a navigable connection between the Pacific and Atlantic Oceans, whose entrance on the Pacific side was between latitudes 47°N and 48°N. It seems that the story at the time did not produce much, if any, reaction on the part of Spanish authorities, or on the part of scholars, nor did it do so for many years afterwards.

Much careful research on the matter of Lok's story has been carried out, but no corroborative evidence has ever been found that such an expedition actually took place. There is no such strait within the quoted latitude range, and many of the details of the account are either unreal or absurd. Nonetheless, it does include a few details that have an intriguing ring of truth, and the fact that between the 48th and 49th parallels there is the broad strait now named after Juan de Fuca, has lent some credence to the possibility that this man took part in a voyage that did discover the entrance to this real strait.

Another account of a voyage across the top of North America was published, again in England, in 1708. The voyage was said to have been made by one Bartholomew de Fonte in 1640; however, most modern historians who have examined the story believe it, with good reason, to be a fabrication.

In any case, the supposed strait between latitudes 47°N and 48°N was delineated, with more or less fanciful detail, in maps of North America and of the Pacific Ocean printed during the second half of the eighteenth century; some of them included expressions to the effect that there was no evidence of the strait's existence, but in other maps it was implied as an established fact.

Because of their interest and the growth in their domains, all three aforementioned empires might have been the first to navigate and establish a presence on the Northwest Coast. Russian ships might have come to it from Asia; Spanish ships from Mexico; and ships belonging to Great Britain might have come directly from their homeland, or from India, or from the ports of Macao and Canton where that nation had shipping facilities. There is even the remote possibility that the coast was first visited in much earlier times by vessels from China. The hard reality, however, is that there is no verified and documented record of an exploration of the Northwest Coast between latitudes 42°N and 56°N, prior to the year 1774.

EARLY EXPLORATIONS OF THE NORTHWEST COAST

The year 1774 marks the beginning of a period of about twenty years in the course of which several nations participated in the exploration and charting of the Northwest Coast of America. The various efforts were not always coordinated and internationally scrutinized, national pride and rivalries intervening, but the end result was a fairly accurate charting of the whole coast. It is remarkable that, given the enormous intricacy of the coastline with its many deep inlets and thousands of offshore islands, only small details were either missed or imperfectly charted.

Spain's participation in this exploratory effort was effected by its Royal Navy, with ships setting out, nearly all, from ports on the Pacific coast of Mexico. Britain participated with two important expeditions of its Royal Navy setting out from the English coast, mainly for the purpose of exploration. In addition, British mariners with either ships of British registry, or ships flying flags of convenience, setting out from different parts of the world, voyaged to the Northwest Coast to trade for sea-otter furs with the Native people in exchange for cheap manufactured goods. For the same purpose, and starting in 1788, ships of the United States of America, then a new nation, whose territory was only on the eastern part of the continent, appeared on the coast.

The conduct of the sea-otter fur trade frequently necessitated visiting previously unknown parts of the coast, and thus effected "discoveries," many of which were divulged and publicised. The participants in the earliest voyages certainly carried maps which would have depicted the **supposed** Juan de Fuca Strait between latitudes 47°N and 48°N.

Both on naval and on trading vessels, the crews were usually exclusively male, but there were a few cases of a vessel having one or more women aboard. Practically all vessels were to a more or less degree armed, and those belonging to one or other of the navies always included some soldiers in their personnel.

The voyagers sought contact with the Native people of the coast for various reasons. In the case of the traders, the motivation was of course finding new partners with which to trade. Europeans did not have the skills required to hunt and trap the fur-bearing animals, particularly the sea otter. Traders also wanted to befriend the Native Americans, to obtain from them fish, water, landing and timber-cutting rights, etc. For the naval vessels, the interest in the local people would have similarly been to barter for food and water, but also to establish political alliances and other useful friendships, and to indulge their curiosity about Native customs, for this was the age of the Enlightenment in Europe. For these various purposes, vessels carried articles considered likely to appeal to the Native people: iron tools, beads, mirrors, metal of different kinds and in different forms, such as nails, knives, etc.

On the whole, contacts between Native people and the newcomers were surprisingly friendly, but there were occasional conflicts and clashes.

Sometimes the Natives pilfered from the foreigners, rather indiscriminately, and there were cases of misappropriation of things extremely valuable to the owners, but practically useless to the pilferers. Sometimes there were misunderstandings of Native customs on the part of the traders, or Native chiefs were insulted, either intentionally or through ignorance. On a few occasions, organized Native groups attacked a vessel for some reason or other. Acts of retaliation for alleged offenses were effected by naval expeditions, but more so by fur traders, and there were cases of totally unjustified abuse by the foreigners.

In these exploratory voyages, requiring crews to spend many months at sea, there were many hazards; illness was common, scurvy for example was still occurring, although beginning to become rare, particularly aboard the British vessels. Ship commanders and pilots had to assess or calculate latitudes and longitudes; the latter requiring much skill with sextants and chronometers for good results. The matter had a bearing on coastal surveying and charting. The naval expeditions were duty-bound to chart as correctly as possible the coasts they examined, and to report on their findings, events, experiences of the respective voyages, including descriptions of places visited and the customs of the local inhabitants. Personnel of fur-trading ships might also chart the coast and write about their respective voyages for the benefit of other traders and colleagues who were to follow.

Contemporary charts, maps, journals, log books, and other documents, concerning these voyages have survived. On specific matters or events, the various sources, taken together, may present a coherent picture, perhaps one report mentioning an important detail not found in any other, but there are conflicting accounts of the same events.

The commanders of these vessels, whether naval or civilian, often assigned names to topographic features. Some commanders refrained from naming a feature known to have been previously named by another commander; some renamed the place anyway if the other commander was of a different nationality; and some, on occasion, renamed a feature even in spite of its original name having being conferred by a compatriot. Occasionally, names were changed in the home country of the explorers, by the authorities, or by cartographers. These various practices resulted in some topographic features appearing under two or more names in different maps or charts of the period.

It is very natural that the coast and some features pertaining to it were initially imperfectly delineated on maps and charts. The identification of the real parts or features can range from perfectly easy to incredibly complicated.

In this work, an interesting case of very inaccurate charting, shortly afterward corrected, is mentioned and briefly analyzed.

In the course of time, the pertinent governmental institutions of Canada and the United States decided upon the toponyms that are now official.

Sequence of events

Below are brief references to events occurring between 1774 and 1790 which have a bearing on the earliest recorded exploration and charting of the area around the present-day city of Vancouver.

Years *1774-75*
- From the port of San Blas, on the Mexican Pacific coast, the Spanish Navy reconnoitre, very succinctly, parts of the western coast of Vancouver Island.

1778
- Captain James Cook of the British Navy on his third voyage around the world "discovers" Nootka Sound.

1785-86
- Ships, most of them owned by British citizens, engage in acquiring sea-otter pelts from the Nuu-chah-nulth people of Nootka Sound and several other parts of the Northwest Coast.

1787
- British fur-trader Captain Charles Barkley (or Barclay) reaches, at latitudes 48°36'N to 48°23'N, longitude 124°45'W, the entrance to the strait that separates Vancouver Island from the mainland territories further south. He assumes this is the strait supposedly discovered by Juan de Fuca, but he does not enter it. In his journal he refers to it as "the long lost Straits of Juan de Fuca."

  News of this event spreads fast, and this **real** strait comes to be called the Juan de Fuca Strait.

1788
- British fur-trader Charles Duncan observes the western entrance to the Juan de Fuca Strait and charts it.
- British fur-trader John Meares leads an expedition that eventually creates a well-documented furore at Nootka. A longboat manned by thirteen expedition men enters the Juan de Fuca Strait, is furiously attacked by Natives shooting arrows, and some crewmen are wounded.

1789

- An expedition of the Spanish Royal Navy (Martínez) spends about six months at Nootka, where it seizes ships belonging to Meares and his associates, and takes steps toward forming an establishment. From Nootka, the expedition's officer José María Narváez, commanding a schooner, voyages to the entrance of the Juan de Fuca Strait but goes no farther.
- The American fur-trader Robert Gray, commanding the schooner *Washington* effects two round trips from Nootka. In the course of the first, between April 14 and April 22, he enters the Juan de Fuca Strait but he too does not travel far inside it.[6]

Circumstances and events in 1790

It is reasonable to believe that, long before the year 1790, the Native people of Nootka and its environs were well aware of the existence and the size of Vancouver Island and of what is now called the Strait of Georgia. However, thus far, this reality had not been ascertained by the foreign mariners for themselves, and it was of course unknown to the world at large.

In 1790, a Spanish naval and military force continued the work of the previous year in building a naval outpost at Nootka. During the summer, Manuel Quimper left Nootka to reconnoitre the whole of the Juan de Fuca Strait, at the eastern end of which he sighted channels leading north. The ship's pilot, Gonzalo López de Haro, charted an area that covers, roughly, the southwestern coast of Vancouver Island and the whole of the Strait, and on it he marked an entrance labelled *Canal de López de Haro* that corresponds, roughly, to the present-day Haro Strait.

John Meares, during a stay in Macao and Canton gathered much information, and some misinformation, about the seizure of his company's ships at Nootka and about recent explorations of the Northwest Coast. Somehow or other he formed a very erroneous notion about the aforementioned trips of the schooner *Washington*. He subsequently moved to London, England where he delivered memoranda and other messages to the British government, thereby initiating a confrontation between Great Britain and Spain over the seizure and their

---

[6] Actually the ship's name was *Lady Washington*, after the wife of the then President of the United States, but in most documents the name appears as *Washington* only.

respective claims of sovereignty on the Northwest Coast. To support his cause, Meares wrote a book, illustrated with drawings and cartography, reporting on his voyages and related matters. Its publication was supported by eminent personages in Britain, and a French edition was published in Paris the following year.

The book includes a long digression affirming that the northern inter-oceanic navigable passage sought by some European countries did exist. The text of the book, as well as one of its maps, assumed the existence of what was called a "Northern Archipelago" and of an inner sea stretching, roughly, from "John de Fuca's Straits" at latitude 48°30 'N, to about latitude 55°20 'N, and reaching far to the eastward. In the map, the shape of the western coast of Vancouver Island and the entrance to the "Straits" are represented, and the location of what is now the city of Vancouver is shown, not as territory belonging to the mainland, but as the waters of an inner sea.

The book, as well as one of Meares' messages to the British government, included words to the effect that the during the year 1789 the vessel *Washington*, commanded by Gray, had

> entered the Straits of John [sic] de Fuca...and penetrating up them, entered into an extensive sea, where she steered to the Northward and Eastward, and had communication with the various tribes who inhabit the shores of the numerous islands that are situated at the back of Nootka Sound,

and that the vessel

> did re-enter the Pacific Ocean between latitude 54°N and 55°N, and... ascertained that Nootka Sound and all the lands adjacent to be an Archipelago of Islands, and not the Continent of America.

The aforementioned map shows an imaginary track of the schooner *Washington* with no indication that it was imagined or supposed (see Plate 5).

Meares' fictitious map may well have been a synthesis of charts by the fur-traders Dixon and Duncan. Dixon's chart of the Queen Charlotte Islands and what is now called Queen Charlotte Sound, was shown with modest accuracy, while the chart by Duncan indicated that from the entrance to the Juan de Fuca Strait, the Pacific waters run eastward for a considerable distance. Taken together, and just possibly with only-imperfectly-understood information from the Native people, these two charts might suggest the possibility that there was a navigable connection between the Juan de Fuca Strait and parts further north.

This probably contributed to the fact that Meares' assertions and map received much credence, and that the British government took them seriously.

Although Dixon, who was an experienced traveller to the Northwest Coast, publicly expressed in England his disbelief in a number of Meares' assertions, there was at the time nobody in Great Britain, nay, in the whole of Europe, with sufficient knowledge of the geographic and historical realities to be able to refute Meares on these matters.

*****

By the end of 1790 much of the shorelines of the Juan de Fuca Strait and of the southern part of the San Juan Islands had been charted, but no vessel from overseas, no Europeans, had been in the waters to the north of these islands, in what came to be called the Strait of Georgia, where the present-day city of Vancouver is located. The first to do so were two vessels manned by members of a Spanish expedition commanded by Francisco de Eliza, in the course of the following year.

Chapter 4

ELIZA EXPEDITION - 1791

On March 26, 1791, the naval officer Francisco de Eliza, then commander of the Spanish establishment at Nootka, received orders from his superiors to undertake a voyage of exploration to parts of the Northwest Coast between latitudes 41°N and 60°N which had not hitherto been carefully surveyed by Spanish navigators. One of the parts was to be the "inside" of the Juan de Fuca Strait, which the officer Quimper had explored the previous year. Eliza was to sail directly from Nootka to latitude 60°N and thence start exploring the coast, on a southward progression. In the places where he would land he was to examine the flora, fauna, metals, stones, character and number of Indians and of strangers, etc. Although fulfilling very little of this ambitious program, explorations were made by an expedition led by Eliza with the participation of the naval officers Juan Carrasco, José María Narváez, Juan Pantoja, and José Antonio Verdía.

The firsthand information that we have about this expedition consists of the manifests of the two vessels used, and three other documents. The principal document is a report by Eliza, which contains little in the way of observations made by Eliza himself, but which consolidates the reports of those officers that did engage actively in the exploration. The other two documents are a brief account by Carrasco, and a report by Pantoja, both of which contain revealing details. Unfortunately, there are no surviving written accounts from either Narváez or from Verdía.

Most of the existing findings of the expedition are to be found in the charts they produced. One of them was apparently drawn by Narváez, Pantoja, and perhaps Eliza, all working together at Nootka at the conclusion of the expedition. It includes all the coasts explored by the expedition and some contiguous ones. For the sake of convenience I call it the Eliza chart.[7]

Of course, all of these documents are written in Spanish. English translations, plus additional information, cartography, explanations and comments, are provided by the American scholar Henry R. Wagner in his book *Spanish Explorations in the Strait of Juan de Fuca*, published in 1933, which does not deal exclusively with this Strait, but with all the bodies of water surrounding Vancouver Island. Some information about the Eliza expedition, and in particular about cartography emanating from it, also appears in Wagner's book *Cartography of the Northwest Coast of America*, published in 1938.

*****

The vessels used for the expedition were a packetboat (Spanish *paquebot*, essentially a frigate but with more cargo space and less heavy armament), a schooner (Spanish *goleta*), and a longboat or launch (Spanish *lancha*).

The packetboat called *San Carlos*, was commanded by Eliza. This ship had at least one smaller boat[8] in addition to the longboat which was carried on board whenever it was not needed. At the outset the personnel consisted of ninety-four men, including a surgeon and a Roman Catholic chaplain.[9]

---

[7] There are at least five copies of this chart, with a few differences in toponyms:

(1) one of large size, very elaborate, now kept in the Naval Museum in Madrid. It has some inset charts of different ports. It has beautiful calligraphy and other details, suggesting that it was meant as the definitive chart of the exploration. The Naval Museum has a second rougher copy;

(2) a similar one now kept at the Library of Congress in the capital of the USA;

(3) a rough chart in the pages of Pantoja's report;

(4) a chart drawn in San Blas by Gonzalo López de Haro in 1792.

They all have long titles and for this reason I do not quote them here, but they can be found in Wagner's books.

[8] Eliza's report contains two statements that prove that they had a boat for use when the longboat was away. This would have been needed for trips ashore. I have not described the *San Carlos* in more detail because it did not visit the Strait of Georgia.

[9] A manifest of *San Carlos* and *Santa Saturnina* reporting details of their personnel at the time they set out from Nootka, reveals that the *San Carlos* had a crew of 87, plus 7 servants (that is, a total of 94 men) and *Santa Saturnina* had a crew of 22.

In a reference to an unspecified stage of the voyage Eliza's report mentions that

The schooner's name was *Santa Saturnina* (alias *Horcasitas* or *Orcasitas)*, details of the dimensions of which are given in some documents of that time.[10] In 1972, resulting from a very careful study, Malcolm Hall Kenyon provided details of this vessel's probable shape, assessments of its dimensions expressed in modern units of measurement, and a reconstruction drawing, a copy of which is included as Plate 5 of this work. According to Kenyon, the schooner's hull "in plain view would have looked like a half walnut," and it "probably had only one continuous deck, high bulwarks (due to the proximity of the main deck to the water line) and possibly a rudimentary cabin aft."

Length of main deck	- 10.85 m
Length of keel	- 9.72 m

The expedition's records reveal that it drew very little water, and its deck had some sort of fireplace for cooking purposes. Eliza claimed that it was known "from experience" that its structure could withstand attacks from Natives throwing spears. Initially its crew totalled twenty-two men, but it had more during at least one of the exploratory excursions.

Santa Saturnina carried victuals for twenty days for the 32 men that were manning this vessel and the longboat [with the implication that *Santa Saturnina* had no room for more than that amount of victuals].

In connection with the periods of time *San Carlos* spent at Esquimalt Harbour and at Port Discovery while the schooner and the longboat were away, Eliza's report mentions that *San Carlos* personnel consisted of 70 men.

Pantoja's report has a statement to the effect that a total of 40 men were engaged in the exploration effected by means of *Santa Saturnina* and the longboat, between June 14 and 24. This is the only specification in the extant data of the composition of groups engaged in exploratory trips.

Since there is no clear explanation on the matter, I venture this possible explanation: the total number of men on the expedition was 116; when at sea, the *San Carlos* carried 94 men, but less when at anchor; when not engaged in exploration, *Santa Saturnina* had 22 men aboard; when so engaged, it had up to 10 extra men drawn from *San Carlos*; the longboat, which was equipped with 13 oars, had a crew of 14 drawn from the other vessels; during the trip of June 14 to 24 led by Narváez and Pantoja, with *Santa Saturnina* and the longboat, the total number of participants was 40; the same was probably true for the exploration of July 1 to 22 effected by Narváez and Verdía; on both occasions, *San Carlos*, was left with a total of about 70 men, plus the 7 servants, first at Esquimalt Harbour and subsequently at Port Discovery.

[10] Small schooners have two masts (larger ones have more) rigged as most modern sailing ships are, as opposed to the old square rigs which had spars supporting the heads of the sails. The main mast of a schooner is always as tall as, or taller, than the foremast.

The <u>longboat</u> had a sail and thirteen oars.[11] There is no specification as to the size of its crew when navigating, though we can surmise that it had thirteen rowers and a commander.

Both *San Carlos* and *Santa Saturnina* had artillery and weaponry. Evidently some of it was transferred to the longboat when it was sent on an excursion. The expedition had a total of 116 men, including eight soldiers belonging to a unit of the Spanish army known as Company of Volunteers from Catalonia, which had been serving at Nootka. The officers Narváez, Carrasco, Pantoja, and Verdía took turns in serving as pilots on the packetboat and in manning the other two craft.

The expedition carried articles intended for giving to people who might be encountered during the voyage, either as presents or in barter. It sailed from Nootka on May 4, 1791. According to Eliza's report, they aimed to start exploring to the northward as instructed but were soon faced with adverse winds. The schooner made too much leeway and failed to keep pace with the packetboat and so he decided to explore instead to the southward. We do not know if these were the real reasons for the change in plans, but regardless, the expedition in fact only explored to the south of Nootka.

The exploration was facilitated by the following facts and circumstances:
* two years earlier, the officer Narváez had journeyed between Nootka and the Juan de Fuca Strait;
* the previous year, the officer Carrasco had participated in the exploration carried out by Quimper, and had therefore covered much of Clayoquot Sound and the Juan de Fuca Strait;
* the officer López de Haro, who had also participated in Quimper's exploration, had drawn a chart covering much of the western coast of Vancouver Island, and the whole of the Juan de Fuca Strait, albeit rather roughly;
* Eliza and a good many of his fellow voyagers had been at Nootka for about thirteen months, and it seems likely that some of them had picked up some words and expressions of the local language. Although Nootkan is quite different from the Salish spoken both around the Juan de Fuca Strait and the

---

[11] Eliza's report says that "*la lancha boga 13 remos*" (the longboat carries 13 oars), an odd number; this seems surprising in that boats usually have an even number of oars.

Strait of Georgia, it is possible that some of the Natives they were about to meet were bi- or multilingual.

López de Haro's chart delineated, albeit incorrectly, the coast between Nootka and Juan de Fuca Strait, as well as the whole of this strait, and specified by name a number of sites. The Eliza expedition made use of seven of these sites. The following list has their present official names and the names they bear in the López de Haro chart and in what is called the Eliza chart. The sequence corresponds to the chronological sequence of events.

Official Name	In López de Haro chart of 1790	In Eliza chart of 1791
Clayoquot Sound	Puerto de Cayucla o de Haro	Archipelago de Clayocuat
Barkley Sound	Bahía de Carrasco	Archipielago de Nitinat o de Carrasco
Esquimalt Harbour	Puerto de Córdova	Puerto de Córdova
Haro Strait	Canal de López de Haro	Canal de López de Haro
Rosario Strait	Boca de Fidalgo	Canal de Fidalgo
Port Discovery	Puerto Quadra	Puerto Quadra
Neah Bay	Bahía de Núñez Gaona	Bahía de Núñez Gaona

Clayoquot and Clayocuat are native synonyms; Haro and Carrasco, surnames of Spanish explorers. In Spanish, o means "or." "Barkley" is now the official spelling, but "Barclay" appears in old texts and charts.

FIRST EXPLORATIONS

Virtually all of the actual explorations of the Eliza expedition were undertaken by means of the *Santa Saturnina* and the longboat, while the *San Carlos*, always with Eliza in command, lay at anchor at some convenient harbour, or moved to another place for a rendezvous.

The first explorations were made at Clayoquot Sound, where Narváez and Carrasco, separately, reconnoitred different parts. Narváez, with the *Santa Saturnina*, devoted six days to the task. Carrasco, commanding the longboat, devoted eight days, and at some stage he was harassed by Natives. Subsequently, Narváez, with the *Santa Saturnina*, explored Barkley Sound, where he had difficulties with Natives who proved to be aggressive and prone to pilfering. On two occasions, groups of over two hundred men, paddling canoes, moved toward the vessel in an aggressive manner, and Narváez held them off by firing his guns, presumably deliberately aimed so that they would not cause casualties as none were reported.

While the *Santa Saturnina* was still at Barkley Sound, the *San Carlos* and the longboat sailed to Esquimalt Harbour, on the southeastern tip of Vancouver Island, arriving on May 29. This was the region of the Haro Strait, the San Juan Islands, and of other straits leading northward to the body of water that came to be called the Strait of Georgia. As far as can be ascertained, this strait had never been visited by persons from overseas, had never been plied by any sailing vessel, and had only been frequented by canoes manned by people from this part of the world. The Eliza expedition was about to initiate a survey of its coasts, while meanwhile in England, John Meares was falsely asserting that the vessel *Washington* had already navigated through these parts on its way to the north.

For exploration purposes the weather must have been an extremely important factor, but, unfortunately, only one reference to it appears in the expedition's records, namely, a statement in Pantoja's report to the effect that the weather was "inconsistent," particularly during June and July, with more days of rain and heavy squalls than days of fair weather. This must have influenced visibility during the explorations that were carried out.

On May 31, while the *San Carlos* remained at Esquimalt, an exploratory trip was attempted by Verdía, with some companions, probably up to fourteen, using the longboat, duly armed. Setting out from that harbour, they began to explore Haro Strait, but were opposed by a large number of Natives in canoes—well armed with bows, arrows, and long spears—shooting arrows toward the longboat. Verdía discharged an unspecified number of firearms shots at them, but, noticing that they paid little attention to this, and that their numbers continued to increase, he withdrew. According to Pantoja's report, some Natives were killed, but apparently there were no casualties on the Spanish side.

The exploring party, with the longboat, returned to Esquimalt Harbour late that same day, rejoining *San Carlos* and its crew.

They remained there until, on June 11, Narváez, with the *Santa Saturnina*, arrived. It is fair to assume that Eliza and his officers then reviewed what they had so far discovered, and discussed how the expedition should proceed. Thus far, in three different places, namely, Clayoquot Sound, Barkley Sound, and the Haro Strait, the expedition had been faced with hostility on the part of the Indigenous people, a fairly good indication that these people disapproved of strangers coming into their territory. It seems probable that this caused the Eliza expedition to be very cautious in their further contacts with the Natives. In any case, henceforth, no trips were to be undertaken with an unaccompanied schooner or longboat.

In the course of June and July, two exploratory excursions were made, both with the schooner and the longboat sailing together.

For the first excursion, the schooner was commanded by Narváez, and the longboat by Pantoja, whose report states that the schooner was supplied "with twenty-five shots for the six cannon and the swivel gun it carried," and that the two crews consisted of their respective commanders plus "thirty sailors, and eight able-bodied and spirited soldiers of the volunteers from Catalonia." That is, a total of forty men.

This excursion took place between June 14 and June 24. Setting out from Esquimalt Harbour, the participants surveyed Haro Strait and its vicinity, encountered many navigational difficulties, but had no further confrontation with the Natives, and sighted, to the north, a very broad and long strait which Pantoja designated as *Gran Canal de Nuestra Señora del Rosario la Marinera*, that is "Great Channel of Our Lady of the Rosary, the Mariner."[12] Could such a long toponym become widely accepted, and endure the test of time? Surely not. It was almost immediately shortened in Spanish documents[13] and the following year was superseded by Vancouver's designation, the Gulph (Gulf) of Georgia.

---

[12] The Spanish word "canal" has the meaning of both "channel" and "canal." In 18th-century English the word "canal" also had the additional meaning of "channel."

[13] In such charts and reports, the words *La Marinera* are dropped. In Vancouver's atlas the designation *Canal de Neiestra Senora del Rosario* (sic) is applied to what is now called Malaspina Strait. Vancouver's book renders "Our Lady" as *Neustra Signora*, while Baker's chart shows, apart from the missing tilde, the correct *Nuestra Senora*.

Shortly after, on the discovery that the gulf was in fact a strait leading back to the open sea, it acquired its present name, the <u>Strait of Georgia</u>. Pantoja charted the coasts that he and Narváez visited, and although his sketch no longer exists, this work must have been incorporated into the Eliza chart.

NARVAEZ-VERDIA EXPLORATION

On June 24, the *Santa Saturnina* and the longboat returned to Esquimalt Harbour, rejoining the *San Carlos*. It was then decided to reconnoitre the *Gran Canal*, that is the Strait of Georgia. According to Eliza's report, he wanted to take part in this task with the packetboat *San Carlos* under his command, but his officers dissuaded him, arguing that this vessel was too bulky and otherwise unsuited for the kind of very risky navigation that this exploration would entail. He then considered participating by commanding *Santa Saturnina* but, finally, he did not do so because, so he said, he had fallen ill. Pantoja's report mentions the reasoning concerning the participation of the *San Carlos*, but not the point about Eliza having "fallen ill." In any case, the assignment for the next exploration was given to José María Narváez and Antonio José Verdía. Because it was to start from *Boca de Fidalgo*, that is the Rosario Strait, the whole expedition moved to a place relatively near to it, Port Discovery on the Olympic Peninsula, the *Puerto de Quadra* of Eliza's report. Their arrival there was on June 29, 1791.

San Carlos, with Eliza and most of the expedition's personnel, remained at this port, while Narváez, commanding the *Santa Saturnina*, assisted by Verdía in command of the longboat, set out provided with food and drink for about twenty days. The records do not specify what equipment the vessels had, or the number of the crew, but presumably the participants included several soldiers, and the total was about forty men as in the case of the previous excursion, which had also been led by Narváez.

It would have been normal practice for Narváez and Verdía to have recorded their trip by means of at least one written report and a sketch of their findings, but there is no evidence that they did so. The existing information concerning their efforts is minimal, and is all secondhand: a few sentences in Eliza's report; and slightly more information in Pantoja's report. In terms of cartography, the only contribution is the pertinent part of the Eliza chart. It is fair to assume that this particular part was drawn by Narváez, perhaps from a now-lost sketch drawn during the trip.

The excursion lasted twenty-one days, and, as suggested by the aforementioned statement of Pantoja about weather, it may have been marred by predominantly bad weather. Setting out from Discovery Bay on July 1,[14] Narváez surveyed the coasts of the short lane now called Rosario Strait (in recognition of the toponym bestowed by Pantoja), Lummi Island, and Bellingham Bay. Both Eliza's and Pantoja's reports, without specifying the dates, reveal that eight days were spent on the waters of the *Gran Canal*, that is, the Strait of Georgia, reaching latitude 50°N. These reports, together with the Eliza chart, indicate that the exploring group formed a rough idea of the intricate complex of coasts that constitute the southern part of the Strait of Georgia, including the site where the city of Vancouver would eventually develop.

Eliza chart, Narváez sketch

One of the interesting details of the Eliza chart is that it is marked with tiny squares at various places onshore, and with tiny anchors at sea near to shorelines. An inscription on the chart states that the tiny squares represent Native villages, and the anchor signs represent "good" anchorages. The chart also has dotted lines, flanking shorelines, and it is clear that they represent shoals or sand banks. However, since dotted lines in other charts represented tracks of vessels in navigation, these lines of the Eliza chart may be misunderstood. The eminent historian Wagner was in error when he wrote in his books that the dotted lines in the Eliza chart represent ship tracks. Unfortunately, the only existing records contain no details of the track of the *Santa Saturnina* and the longboat during this excursion.

The part of the Eliza chart that represents the area of the present-day city of Vancouver and its vicinity has been identified by reference to longitudes and latitudes indicated on the chart itself, and by other connotations. In this work, and merely for the sake of convenience, I refer to this part of the chart as the Narváez sketch.

---

[14] June 30, according to Pantoja, July 1 according to Eliza and Carrasco. I guess Pantoja was wrong on this, although confusion sometimes arose because the navigational day started at noon.

Plate 6 in this work has a copy of this sketch plus a note in which the abbreviated toponyms are explained. Plate 7 has a chart of the same area, as drawn in the near-perfect cartography of our time. Even a cursory inspection of these two plates reveals that the Narváez sketch is a very inaccurate depiction of the site, and this raises the question of why Narváez and Verdía made the mistakes that they did. The sketch has nine toponyms; six of them are spelled with abbreviations that would be easily understood by persons with a knowledge of Spanish. The following are these toponyms spelt out in full: *Punta de San José, Punta de San Rafael, Boca de Florida Blanca, Punta de la Bodega, Bocas del Carmelo, Rio de la Aguada, Islas de Apodaca, Isla(s) de Lángara, Isla de Zepeda.*[15]

Eliza's report mentions only three of these toponyms, and Pantoja's report mentions only one of these three. Neither document provides any topographic detail concerning any of them.

A few persons interested in the history and the cartography of this part of Canada have analyzed the sketch and formulated assertions and presumptions on the identification of the topographic features, villages, and anchorages shown. The earliest, important contribution to the subject is Wagner's book on the Spanish explorations. His subsequent book *Cartography*, makes a further contribution, and in a few cases, it contains assertions and conjectures that differ from those in his earlier book. Wagner was not a resident of this area and he admitted that he was not sufficiently acquainted with its geography, habitat, or history to be very firm in some of his opinions, and he expressed satisfaction that persons more and better acquainted should have and express different opinions.

Two outstanding residents of the area who wrote and published something on the matter, from about 1937, are the magistrate and historian F.W. Howay, and the then head of the Vancouver City Archives, Major J.S. Matthews. Howay made only a few pronouncements, but Matthews undertook to publicize Narváez' exploration, and in so doing he was carried away to make assertions that have absolutely no documentary or cartographic basis.

---

[15] Some copies of the sketch are inscribed *"Islas bajas y anegades"* (low-lying and waterlogged islands) at the point where the north arm of the Fraser reaches the sea to the south of Point Grey.

What is clear enough, and virtually agreed by Wagner, Howay, and Matthews, is that:

- *Punta de San José* is Birch Point on the south side of Semiahmoo Bay;
- *Punta de San Rafael* is Kwomais Point at Ocean Park in Surrey;
- *Isla de Zepeda* (Zepeda Island) is a misconception of the peninsula of Point Roberts which was envisaged as an island;
- *Isla(s) de Lángara* corresponds either to the promontory of Point Grey alone, or to Point Grey, Sea Island, Lulu Island, and nearby islets;
- the bold line between *Isla de Zepeda* and *Isla(s) de Lángara* represents the coast between Point Roberts and Point Grey, and openings indicate the several outlets of the Fraser River;
- the dotted lines running between the western tip of *Isla de Zepeda* and the north of *Isla(s) de Lángara* represent the shoals now called Roberts Bank and Sturgeon Bank;
- the three tiny squares shown at the site of the supposed *Isla(s) de Lángara*, indicate the village called *Eyalmu* that existed on the site now known as Jericho Beach;
- *Islas de Apodaca* (Apodaca Islands) represent Bowen Island and its nearby islets;
- *Bocas del Carmelo* (Carmelo mouths) represent the entrances to Howe Sound.

One detail worth noting here is that Matthews appears to have assumed, without comment, that the names *Isla(s) de Lángara* (Point Grey and other islands?) and *Islas de Apodaca* (Bowen, Pasley, and possibly Keats Islands) referred in each case to only one island. In the case of Point Grey, this assumption is possibly correct, possibly not, in that in some copies of the sketch, the designation is singular (*Isla* written in the old-fashioned way *Ysla* abbreviated to *Y*^{a}), and in others it is plural (*Islas* written in the old-fashioned way *Yslas* abbreviated to *Y*^{s}). No such inconsistency exists for Bowen Island where the original Spanish designation is always plural and presumably therefore referred to all the islands at the mouth of Howe Sound, and not Bowen Island alone.

Other points are less clear. What village, for example, is meant by the two tiny squares on a promontory to the east of *Islas de Apodaca*? In Major Matthews opinion, the symbols represent the village that existed at *Stuck-ale*, near Cypress Creek; that is, the terrain at the mouth of that creek, where there was, for some years, an important fish cannery. However, the shape and location of the two square dots suggest to me that they may represent the village known to have existed on the western tip of Horseshoe Bay.

The identity of *Punta de la Bodega* (Bodega Point) and the three tiny squares marked on it is problematic. Wagner asserted that the spot was "evidently" Point Atkinson, that is what is now Lighthouse Park in West Vancouver. Matthews affirmed that the *punta* was Ferguson Point in Stanley Park, and that the tiny squares represent the Squamish village of *Homulchesun* (*Wh'mullutsthun, Whu-mul-chits-tun*), known to have existed near the mouth of Capilano Creek. This opinion seems to imply that Narváez envisaged the terrain of the park as belonging to the north shore of Burrard Inlet. I have no firm opinion on this question.[16]

What would be the reason for the Eliza chart showing the peninsulas of Point Roberts and Point Grey as being islands? The Spanish officers Alcalá Galiano and Valdés who explored this same coastal region the following year eliminated some of the possibilities when they observed both at close quarters. To them, the peninsulas appeared just as they do today.

Boca de Florida Blanca

Some rather astonishing features of what may be called the Narváez sketch (as part of the Eliza chart) are: the broad opening labelled *Boca de Florida Blanca*, the bold line and dotted line connecting it with *Punta de San Rafael*, and the space between this promontory and *Isla de Zepeda*. These parts of the sketch suggest that:

- the space between Boundary Bay and Burrard Inlet appeared to Narváez <u>not</u> as land, but as an inner sea;
- somewhere in the vicinity of the Indian Arm of Burrard Inlet, or maybe the Pitt River, he sighted the mouth (*boca*) of a very broad inlet or channel whose shores ran in a northeasterly direction.

This later feature, surely, is the most puzzling part of the sketch, in that it might be assumed to indicate a navigable lane penetrating deeply into the mainland, but there is absolutely nothing of the sort at that location. As mentioned below and in Appendix 3, the name of the entrance of this supposed strait or inlet *Boca de Florida Blanca* has a somewhat interesting history.

---

[16] N.A. Doe has completed a computer-aided analysis of the errors in the Eliza chart and considers the odds to be slightly in favour of the Stanley Park identification.

It is clear that the line the sketch shows between *Punta de San José* and *Punta de San Rafael* represents the shores of Semiahmoo Bay from Birch Point, around Drayton Harbor, past Blaine and White Rock, to Kwomais Point. The chart has, just off that coastline, an anchor that suggests that the explorers anchored the *Santa Saturnina* and the longboat there, and a notation indicating that they made and recorded observations of compass or magnetic variation. A Native village is also marked at the mouth of the Campbell River, just east of present-day White Rock. Taken together, this evidence reveals that the Spaniards must have spent some time in the vicinity of Boundary Bay. How close did they actually get to the bay's shore? The observations of Vancouver and Galiano who visited the area eleven months later suggest very definitely that these explorers found its appearance to be roughly as it is now. The shore was edged by a very wide shoal that would impede close approach by vessels such as those used by Narváez and Verdía. Evidently, the two Spaniards:

- sighted, from a considerable distance to the south, the promontories now called Kwomais Point and Point Roberts;
- failed to observe the shoreline of Mud Bay and Boundary Bay;
- formed the impression that the terrain to the north of the shore, the modern Delta and Richmond areas of the Lower Mainland, was covered by water.

Could there be a plausible explanation for this misconception?

Over the years several have been suggested, but one of the difficulties we now have is that there is no way of knowing for sure what the river and its delta looked like more than two hundred years ago. Modern flood-control measures have eliminated the once annual floods that inundated the area during early summer when the snow in the mountains begins to melt in earnest.

One supposition is that in July 1791, the Fraser and Pitt Rivers had such an extraordinarily high freshet that their waters flooded Douglas Island and the flatland of North and South Delta. If this was the case, the mariner José Maria Narváez, then 26 years old, might have climbed the tallest mast of *Santa Saturnina* in order to scan the horizon, and gained the impression that the surface of South Delta, Lulu Island, North Delta, and lowland Surrey, was an inner sea, and that the space of Douglas Island, where those two rivers join, was the opening to a broad water lane. Is such a possibility justifiable in the light of the topography of the whole area? Unfortunately not. The hills of upland Surrey make it impossible to see as far as Douglas Island from anywhere in Boundary Bay.

Other suggestions are offered by White Rock resident, Nicholas Doe who has been studying the late 18th-century cartography of the area. He suggests:

Although it is possible that flooding in the Fraser Delta deceived Narváez into thinking that there was a passage to the north between Point Roberts (*Isla de Zepeda*) and Kwomais Point (*Punta de San Rafael*), there are other possibilities. Point Roberts as seen from the eastern and southern sides of Boundary Bay frequently appears to be an island even when the river is not in flood.

The land around the northern shore of the bay is very low-lying compared to the fifty-metre-high sandstone cliffs at Point Roberts. The Fraser River once discharged into Boundary Bay and, but for modern dredging and diking, this land would still be an active part of the Fraser's floodplain which extends about twenty kilometres to the north. The lack of height of the shore above the level of the sea is particularly striking nowadays because the hinterland is farmland and the skyline is only occasionally marked by clumps of trees or man-made structures such as farm buildings and power-transmission lines. Judging by the remarks of European explorers in the fur-trade era, the Boundary Bay coast beyond a narrow fringe of saltmarshes was originally "wooded," most probably by thickets of shrubs such as willow, red alder, crab-apple, etc. These could possibly have made the land more visible from a distance than the present-day fields which are only just above sea level; however, Captain Vancouver in 1792, also remarked on the conspicuous appearance of Point Roberts compared to the surrounding land. If the Spaniards did not travel far into Boundary Bay, and remained at their anchorage to the south in Semiahmoo Bay, near Birch Point, then the northern shore, about eight nautical miles [15 km] away, might have remained below their horizon.

A second possible reason for them being deceived, is that at almost any time of the year in the Pacific Northwest, whenever it is humid and relatively calm, a thin mist forms just above the surface of the sea. This often obscures the contact point between water and land on distant shorelines, while the higher ground beyond remains visible. In wet weather, Point Roberts can usually be seen through the murk from anywhere in Boundary Bay, as can the northern shore in the direction of Crescent Beach, but to the east of Point Roberts, the shoreline sometimes cannot be seen at all. But for the dike and the structures in the direction of the Delta Air Park, the shoreline could easily be missed.

In the summertime, yet a third common reason for the 'disappearance' of the land is refraction in the heat haze rising from the tidal flats around the bay. If the sun is hot, the sand and mud at the surface of the flats quickly dries out and heats the air which becomes less dense, with the result that the light from the sky is redirected toward the observer, a phenomenon often seen on straight roads on hot days. The effect is very striking and not at all uncommon; the low-lying parts of the north shores of Boundary Bay cannot be seen at all from the south, and the horizon appears very bright.

Since Narváez visited the area in the summer, and since he was so thoroughly deceived, the heat-haze explanation would seem to be the best; however, the heat-haze effect obviously requires hot sunshine. The weather was reported by the Spaniards to be mostly rainy and windy although there must have been some clear sky, as Narváez measured the variation of his compass, albeit incorrectly, in the bay. Another factor which would tend to rule against acceptance of the heat-haze explanation is the tides. The heat-haze effect is most noticeable when the tide is low during the day, which it often is in the summer in this area. However, a tide table I have calculated for White Rock in July 1791 indicates that the first week in July was a period of neap tides and the day-time low tides were actually all fairly high.

While we can never be certain what caused Narváez to make his mistake, I suspect that the visibility of the high land at Point Roberts relative to the very low-lying surrounding land was as likely a cause as any extraordinary degree of flooding.

Narváez was of course not all that wrong; for about five thousand years following the retreat of the glaciers of the last ice-age, Point Roberts was indeed an island out in the Strait of Georgia. Not until then did the sand, silt, and clay sediment from the Fraser River join it to the mainland. Who knows?—perhaps in the centuries to come, global warming and the accompanying rising levels of the sea will return the Point to its island state, and Narváez's error will be rectified.

Regarding the apparent extension of the shoreline toward Indian Arm there is a quite satisfactory explanation for this. The Eliza chart must have been assembled from a collection of sketches and chart segments made by the various navigators on different occasions. One of the jobs of the cartographers who compiled the final version of the chart, probably at Nootka in the fall of 1791, was to reduce all of these fragments to the same scale. Now if you look at the segment of the Eliza chart between Deception Pass (*Boca de Flon*) in present-day Washington, and Kwomais Point (*Punta de San Rafael*), you will notice that that particular segment of the chart is too large. Padilla and Bellingham Bays extend too far east, and Kwomais Point and the coastline north of this, too far north. Careful measurement shows that, according to the final chart's latitude and longitude scales, this whole segment of coastline has been drawn by the cartographers about 60% bigger in each direction than it should have been. Some other segments of the Eliza chart have a similar kind of error. If this mistake is corrected, then it will be found that the supposed shoreline north of Kwomais Point actually follows very closely the border between the ninety-metre-high Sunshine Hills in Delta and the adjacent Fraser lowland, terminating near the present-day Alex Fraser Bridge. This is a natural boundary to have supposed to have existed between land and sea when viewed from a distance to the south. The apparent coincidence of *Boca de Florida Blanca* and the Indian Arm of Burrard Inlet is, in my opinion, nothing more than the result of a silly cartographic scaling error.

If, as seems likely, the eastward trending line from *Punta de la Bodega* (Stanley Park?) is a crude representation of the North Shore Mountains along the northern side of Burrard Inlet, which are highly visible from anywhere in the area and quite possibly also incorrectly transposed from a sketch to the chart, then the *Boca de Florida Blanca* would be no more than a very vague indication of the perceived presence of the Fraser Valley.

*****

Written information

The only existing information of the exploration effected by Narváez and Verdía within the Strait of Georgia is contained in a few sentences in the reports written by Eliza and Pantoja. Except for a few expressions about the shape and trend of the strait and a few details having to do with navigation, all that these two documents state on the matter is copied verbatim in the Appendices of this work. The following are paraphrased English translations.

From Eliza's report

Narváez and Verdía sailed through the *Gran Canal de Nuestra Señora del Rosario* [Strait of Georgia] for eight days, reached the latitude of 50°N, always following its trend, and did no more because they were running short of food. On the shores of the strait they sighted the mouths of some rivers of sweet water. They thought that between *Bocas del Carmelo* [entrance to Howe Sound] and *Punta de la Bodega* there must be a copious river, because, when the schooner was anchored two miles [3.7 km] out,[17] they collected and drank sweet water [obviously meaning water from the sea surface]. However, because of bad weather, they were unable to ascertain whether there really was such a river. In the neighbourhood of *Bocas del Carmelo* and of *Islas de Cepeda* [sic] a large number of Natives, paddling canoes, came forth toward the schooner. At first, the explorers were somewhat alarmed. However, when the Natives came closer, it was found that they did not carry bows and arrows, "but only an abundance of various kinds of fish, among which were very large and delicate salmon." The Spaniards found that the waters of the strait had an abundance of tuna fish[18] and a large number of whales of considerable size.[19]

---

[17] I assume in this work that by a mile, all sailors of whatever nationality, meant a nautical mile. This is the distance covered by one minute of arc of latitude, or 1.852 km. A nautical mile is 15% longer than the land mile (1.609 km), which would have been used, for example, by Simon Fraser.

[18] Tuna are warm-water pelagic fish that are either exceedingly rare in the Strait of Georgia, or never visit it at all. Bones of bluefin tuna and albacore have only been found in ancient archaeological sites on the west coast of Vancouver Island. Eliza must have been referring to some other species.

[19] The Spanish for whales is *ballenas*. The Eliza chart shows as Y^s [*Islas*] *de las Ballenas*, the present-day Ballenas Islands, off the east coast of Vancouver Island, between Parksville and Lantzville. Humpback whales were once very common in the Strait of Georgia. Commercial whaling ceased there in 1908, by which time the stock had been totally eliminated.

From Pantoja's report

Narváez and his companions sailed through the *Gran Canal* (Strait of Georgia) for eight days, reaching the latitude of Nootka before turning back because they were running short of food and the winds were not favourable. On both sides of the Strait, there are very good anchorages, many plots of flat land and an abundance of pasture, quadrupeds and birds, and several streams of fresh water. "Close to Zepeda Island and for a distance of two leagues [11 km] the group sailed through a line of white water that was more sweet than salt." This suggests that there must be a copious river in that vicinity. On the shores of that island there are numerous Indians, much more docile and tractable than those of the entrance to the Strait [either meaning the entrance to the Haro Strait or to the Juan de Fuca Strait, and its vicinity, where a schooner was attacked in 1788].

Immediately following this statement, Pantoja's report has three others that are clumsily worded, and baffling in some respects. Here is the essence of these statements, along with some comments.

1) *Statement:* The Indians of this part speak a language entirely different from those of other parts.

   Comment: The text does not specify the other languages. Actually, there are good reasons to affirm that the only local languages of which these Spaniards could have known enough of for comparison was that of the Nuu-chah-nulth and the Makah, but perhaps they had picked up a few words or expressions of other languages in places where they had met Native people.

2) *Statement:* The Spaniards did not understand the language, but those Indians expressed clearly enough that ships much larger than the *Santa Saturnina* had been in the "Canal."

   Comment: The context seems to imply that the word *Canal* signified the Strait of Georgia, but there is no evidence of any ship having been in the strait prior to the two almost consecutive visits by the *Santa Saturnina*. So, perhaps the Spaniards simply misunderstood what the Indians meant.

3) *Statement:* One of those Indians wore bracelets of very fine brass, which had been engraved, apparently with a burin. He refused to "barter" them. That kind of bracelet had not been seen in the possession of the Indians of the

whole coast, nor among the trifles carried by "foreign" [i.e. non-Spanish] vessels that had been on that coast since the Spaniards first came to it.[20]

Comment: The Galiano expedition's records and several other documents testify to the fact that Natives of this part of the world had copper bracelets made by cold hammering. However, it is obvious that the kind of bracelets with good engravings were not made locally but in some industrialized part of the world. Perhaps they had been acquired from vessels visiting Nootka or other parts of the western coast of Vancouver Island, changed hands by intertribal trade, and eventually came to the area of Point Roberts.

There seems to be a solid base for the conclusion that there was communication by canoe between communities of the coasts of the Strait of Georgia and of the Juan de Fuca Strait. There are also known cases of articles being transported considerable distances, perhaps by successive trading transactions.

Following these three statements, Pantoja's report has another one which includes the notion that some Native people from the mainland, with horses, used to come to the shores of the region of the Juan de Fuca Strait or of the Strait of Georgia to barter for fish before returning home. This statement and related points are cited and commented on in Appendix 5 of this book.

*****

Conjectures about a river

The information from Eliza and Pantoja reveals that their companions Narváez and Verdía believed that there was a major river estuary in the vicinity of the present-day city of Vancouver. According to Eliza's report, these men thought that the mouth of the river was somewhere between *Bocas del Carmelo* and *Punta de la Bodega*, which, in the Eliza chart, are shown as belonging to the coast on the north side of Burrard Inlet. Actually there is no large river debouching into the sea there. Pantoja's report suggests that these men suspected that there was a river estuary somewhere in the vicinity of *Isla de Cepeda*, that is, Point Roberts. This was a much better observation, since the estuary of the Fraser River is in fact just to the north of that point. The line of

---

[20] I submit that this statement in Pantoja's report is inaccurately rendered in Wagner's book *Spanish Explorations in the Strait of Juan de Fuca* and that the translation I give here is correct.

water "more sweet than salt" would have been river water spreading out over the surface of the denser sea water. Neither report makes any mention of the *Boca de Florida Blanca* or makes any statement to the effect that the *Boca* might be the mouth of a major river. However, subsequent developments indicate that this is what came to be thought.[21]

Landings, contacts with Natives

The anchor signs in the Eliza chart suggest that the *Santa Saturnina* and longboat were for some time anchored at some distance to the west of Point Grey (just off Sturgeon Bank) and also near the mouth a of a river that the chart labels *Rio de la aguada*. This later place must be a stream in the vicinity of Howe Sound; perhaps Roberts Creek, Judge Howay suggested. In Spanish nautical terminology, *aguada* means watering place. I conclude therefore that at some time the schooner and longboat were anchored at that place, and that some of the crew went ashore to replenish their supply of fresh water. There is no indication that there was any human habitation there.

Did the Spaniards land anywhere in the Greater Vancouver area? There is not the slightest evidence in the Spanish records that they did so. There is no reference to the nature of the terrain, the flora, or the fauna of the area; their chart is inaccurate and contains nothing that could not have been observed from the sea; all of which strongly suggests that they did not in fact make such a landing.[22] Perhaps, because of the earlier confrontations between Natives and the crews of the schooner and the longboat, Narváez and Verdía were very wary about landing and there was nothing intrinsically interesting to the Spanish about the area that would merit them undertaking risky overland ventures. Their interest was in the to-them-unknown course of the Strait of Georgia.

The Spaniards evidently did have some contact with Native people in the areas of Point Roberts and of Bowen Island in Howe Sound, but the contacts took place on the water, the Natives being in canoes. The Spaniards obtained

---

[21] This notion was probably conveyed to the participants of the Spanish expedition that explored this coast the following year, 1792.

[22] Yet, Major Matthews and other persons have asserted, in spite of the complete lack of evidence for it, that landings were effected in at least two places and, in particular, that the party made a journey from Boundary Bay to the Fraser River.

some salmon. Since the references from Eliza and Pantoja qualify the local salmon as succulent, it was perhaps cooked on the stove that the *Santa Saturnina* had on board.

Near the end of Eliza's report there is a statement, poorly phrased but understandable if read in its context, that in his opinion the *Gran Canal* offered about the only possibility of a passage to the Atlantic Ocean, assuming, he says, that such a passage exists. I am sure that by the expression *Gran Canal*, Eliza meant the *Gran Canal de Nuestra Señora del Rosario*, the Strait of Georgia, not the feature that appears on his chart with the designation *Boca de Florida Blanca*. Surely, there is a great difference between the idea of a great "canal," or "channel," which suggests length, and the idea of mouth, which merely suggests width.[23] Besides, as mentioned above, Eliza's report makes no mention whatsoever of this *boca*.

End of the expedition and sequel

The exploratory excursion carried out by Narváez and Verdía in the *Santa Saturnina* and the longboat ended on July 22, 1791, with their arrival at Port Discovery, where the *San Carlos* had been tarrying. There, the longboat was taken aboard, and the command of the *Santa Saturnina* was transferred to the officer Juan Carrasco, while Narváez and Verdía were transferred to the *San Carlos*.

On July 25 the two vessels left Port Discovery and moved to Neah Bay, where they spent four days, and then departed, bound for Nootka.

San Carlos made the trip and arrived on August 30. However, the schooner, failing to make good progress toward that destination, made for Monterey in California instead, and subsequently moved to San Blas, where Carrasco wrote a brief report, dated November 9, addressed to the viceroy of New Spain, which included some information on the Eliza expedition. About nine days later the viceroy received this report, which provided him with the first news he had had of the expedition.[24]

---

[23] I make this clear because it has been asserted in print that Eliza's report says that this *Boca* might be the opening to an inter-oceanic navigable passage. In fact, the *Boca* is not even mentioned in the report.

[24] Letter from Fidalgo, commander at San Blas, accompanying the report sent to the viceroy.

Cartography

The records of the Eliza expedition are not explicit about the cartographic work it carried out, but from details in the records I deduce the following:

- having a copy of the López de Haro chart drawn the previous year, which showed the coast from Nootka to the east end of the Juan de Fuca Strait, Narváez, Pantoja, and Verdía, explored additional areas not included in that chart and drew up charts of these areas;
- the three officers, on board *San Carlos* during its trip from Port Discovery to Nootka, engaged in piecing together their sketches and the López de Haro chart, as a preliminary to the preparation of a chart of the whole of the southern part of Vancouver Island and its surrounding waters;
- upon the ship's arrival at Nootka, the voyagers learned that a Spanish maritime expedition led by Alejandro Malaspina had just spent two weeks there, in the course of which it had produced the earliest known chart covering the whole of Nootka Sound;
- there, at Nootka, Narváez, Pantoja, and Verdía—perhaps with Eliza's participation—drew the original of what has been called the Eliza chart, which incorporated the new information on Nootka Sound. Pantoja drew a rough copy of this chart and attached it to the end of his report, which he probably wrote at Nootka. Francisco de Eliza wrote, or completed, his report, which is dated October 10, 1791. The Eliza chart and charts of Clayoquot Sound, Barkley Sound, and perhaps of other places, were put in a metal tube, and properly sealed;
- on October 15, *San Carlos*, commanded by Ramón Saavedra, assisted by Juan Pantoja, sailed from Nootka, carrying the tube containing Eliza's report and other papers destined for the viceroy;
- Eliza, Narváez, and Verdía remained at Nootka;
- *San Carlos* arrived at the Mexican port of San Blas on December 22, 1791;
- the tube containing the documents was forwarded to the viceroy's office in Mexico City;
- either the original of the Eliza chart, or else an excellent copy with fine penmanship, was sent to Spain, and is one of those now stored at the Naval Museum in Madrid;
- Pantoja lent his copy of the Eliza chart to Gonzalo López de Haro, who drew a more artistic copy of it, and stated in its cartouche that he produced it in San Blas in January 1792;

- by that time, Viceroy Revillagigedo and Alejandro Malaspina had issued instructions and advice for further exploration of the Juan de Fuca Strait and adjacent waters, as described in the following chapter.

Chapter 5

VANCOUVER AND GALIANO EXPEDITIONS

Facts and circumstances to be described below conspired to produce a very strange situation on the coast in 1792. Two vessels of the British Royal Navy and two of the Spanish Royal Navy were engaged simultaneously in exploring and charting a part of the world, over which each of the respective nations sought dominion and exclusive sovereignty.

Both expeditions reconnoitred the site of the present-day city of Vancouver and its environs. Only some of the members of the British expedition, with two boats, participated, but both Spanish vessels crewed by forty-eight men were involved, and they spent more time in the area than did the British.

THE GEORGE VANCOUVER EXPEDITION

In 1791, under orders from the British government, two ships of the British Royal Navy, *Discovery*, and *Chatham*, were dispatched on a voyage, starting from England, under the overall command of Captain George Vancouver. He was given various assignments, the main ones being to survey the Northwest Coast of America, and to meet at Nootka with a delegate of the Spanish government to arrange implementation of some articles of a convention recently agreed upon by the two governments concerning the Northwest Coast of America and matters related to the aforementioned events at Nootka in 1788 and 1789.

Vancouver had participated in the last of Cook's voyages three famous round-the-world voyages, during which he had spent a month at Nootka Sound, and had undergone training in the complex art of navigation and coastal surveying. He sailed equipped with sextants and chronometers of the best quality, and with as much information as was to be had concerning the explorations carried out along the coast prior to 1790. This information had been gathered from Cook; British fur traders such as Barkley, Duncan, Dixon, and Meares; Spanish mariners; and from others.

The aforementioned erroneous and misleading statements in Meares' book concerning the alleged discoveries of Robert Gray with the vessel *Washington* were taken seriously enough by the British government and its Admiralty to influence the orders issued for Vancouver's expedition, which included the following points:

- he was to examine "the supposed Straits of Juan de Fuca, said to be situated between latitudes 48°N and 49°N, and to lead to an opening through which the sloop *Washington* is reported to have passed in 1789 and to come out again to the northward of Nootka";
- he was to seek accurate information about "any water communication" between the Northwest Coast of America and "the country upon the opposite side of the continent" inhabited by British subjects ("the country" being, of course, Canada situated on the eastern side of the continent);
- since it appeared that the Spanish government was disposed to provide "every assistance and information" to officers of the British Navy employed on the coast, he was required to do everything in his power to cultivate a good understanding with Spanish naval officers he might encounter on the coast in order that he might reap the good effects of this disposition of the Spanish Court;
- if any attack was made on his squadron or on British ships under his protection, he was to resist it to the outmost and ... endeavour to destroy or capture the Vessels making such an attack.

Discovery, ship rigged, 340 tons, carried three boats, had a complement of about a hundred men, and was commanded by Vancouver. *Chatham*, brig rigged, 139 tons, carried two boats and had about eighty-four men, with William Robert Broughton in command. The expedition's equipment included tents for shelter, seine fishing nets, as well as articles to be given to Native people as gifts or in exchange for favours. These included axes, hatchets, adzes, chisels, hawsers, nails, saws, files, rasps, gimlets, pocket knives, spades, shovels, pick axes, sickles, iron bars, brass and copper sheets, buttons, thimbles, frying pans, tin kettles, pots, jugs, scissors, scarlet cloth, feathers, red caps, earrings and beads of different colours.

Since it was clearly expected that the expedition would be engaging in important negotiations with the Spaniards on behalf of the British government, it would have been prudent, one would have thought, for the expedition to have included at least one person who could speak Spanish. However, no such person was deliberately included.

It was also, seemingly, not by virtue of any deliberate decision during the preparatory stages, but by good luck, that the expedition included a few men who were proficient artists. A number of the participants made valuable contributions to the records of the voyage with their sketches of interesting places they visited and things that they saw, with charts and sketch maps, and with journals, letters, or notes about their experiences and observations. Of these documents, the following contain information relevant to the subject of this study: a book written mostly by Vancouver; a journal attributed to Edward Bell; a journal and a rough log by the officer Peter Puget; journals by the officers Thomas Manby and Joseph Baker; and a journal by Archibald Menzies.[25] Of the many charts that the expedition produced, those of the Vancouver area are what I call, for the sake of convenience, the Baker chart and the Vancouver chart (Plates 9 and 10).

From England to the Juan de Fuca Strait

In April, 1791, *Discovery* and *Chatham* departed from the English coast. They sailed around the tip of Africa; crossed the Southern Ocean to Australia and New Zealand; stopped at Tahiti and at the Hawaiian Islands; and then made for the west coast of America, making landfall in mid-April 1792, at a point about 180 kilometres north of San Francisco Bay in California.[26] From there the

---

[25] There is evidence that Broughton kept a journal but it has long been lost. Broughton apparently spoke French and used it to converse with José Mariano Moziño at Nootka.

[26] Since leaving England, Vancouver had kept time by reference to time at Greenwich (Greenwich Mean Time [GMT], now known as Universal Coordinated Time [UTC]). Consequently, upon arriving on the Pacific coast, he reckoned local time to be some 16 hours ahead of Greenwich, and the longitude to be about 240 degrees east. The convention of those on the coast however was the one that we use nowadays, in that local time is reckoned to be about 8 hours behind Greenwich, and the longitude about 120 degrees west. The only difference between these two reckonings is a day difference in the date. Vancouver's dates are one day ahead of those used by the Spaniards, an anomaly that is avoided nowadays by use of an

ships sailed north up the coasts of Oregon and Washington, examining the coast as they went, until they approached the Juan de Fuca Strait.

On April 28, just south of the entrance of the Strait, the Vancouver expedition encountered the vessel *Columbia* and, lo and behold! its captain was the American fur-trader Robert Gray himself. Two of Vancouver's men, Puget and Menzies, went aboard to acquire information. During the conversation with the British visitors, Gray denied that he had ever circumnavigated Vancouver Island, and asserted that all he had done in that area was to penetrate into the strait for "only fifty miles" (93 km) and, not seeing good chances of obtaining furs therein, he had left the same way he had come.[27] Menzies' journal says:

> ...it may appear no less curious than interesting that here, at the entrance of Juan de Fuca Straights [sic] we should meet with the very man whose voyage up in it with the Sloop Washington, as delineated by the fertile fancy of Mr. Meares, gave rise to so much theoretical speculation and chimerical discussion—I say interesting because it enables us to detect to the world a fallacy in this matter which no excuse can justify.

Gray's statements were communicated to Vancouver who, giving them due credit, had little hesitation in branding as disinformation, statements in Meares' book about the seas "at the back of Nootka Sound" and passages to the coast north of latitude 47°N. Vancouver records in his book his rather scathing opinions of what "theoretical geographers have thought proper to assert," and conclusions "not derived from any source of substantial information" concerning "the pretended discoveries of De Fuca and De Fonte," conclusions he goes on to say have been recently "revived in order to prove the existence of a Northwest Passage...." So, Vancouver was now absolutely sure that Gray had not explored Juan de Fuca Strait and further north, but he remained unaware that the Eliza Expedition had done so the previous year.

---

internationally-agreed date-line. In this book, the dates from the Vancouver expedition's records are adjusted as necessary to the now-standard dating by subtracting one day.

[27] Vancouver's journal says "about 50 (nautical) miles"; Menzies' journal says "about 17 leagues." Since a league is about three nautical miles, the two figures are practically identical. Gray had travelled almost exactly half the distance between the entrance of the Strait and its eastern termination near Whidbey Island.

After that important and lucky contact with Gray, the British expedition went on to explore much of the Juan de Fuca Strait, its southern continuation into Admiralty Inlet, and Puget Sound, and parts of the San Juan Island group. Thence they proceeded to the *Gran Canal de Nuestra Señora del Rosario* (the Strait of Georgia) and after surveying its southeastern part, the expedition arrived in June 1792 at Birch Bay, just to the south of the Greater Vancouver area.

THE ALCALA GALIANO EXPEDITION

Meanwhile, the Spanish government had received reports of the expedition led by Manuel Quimper in 1790, which suggested that the Juan de Fuca Strait extended a long way in an east-west direction, and that it might connect to other bodies of water. They also had received reports emanating from England on the activities of the fur traders, particularly details published by Meares in his book. The government, acutely aware of how much their strategic interests could be affected should a navigable passage be discovered from the west all the way to the Atlantic Ocean, ordered the viceroy of New Spain to urgently investigate the claims. As a result, an expedition was dispatched from the port of San Blas to reconnoitre and chart the coast from 56°N southward to San Francisco, including the inner reaches of the Juan de Fuca Strait.

At the time he received this order, the viceroy was unaware that the Eliza expedition had already explored the strait and had discovered channels leading further north. Abiding by his government's order, the viceroy, Revillagigedo, initially assigned the task to the officer Francisco Mourelle, who was given explicit written instructions dated September 9, 1791. Subsequently, the viceroy received reports from the Eliza expedition, and on the advice of Alejandro Malaspina, leader of the Spanish naval expedition that had just been exploring on the Northwest Coast, changed his plans.

The expedition would use two vessels called *Sutil* and *Mexicana*. These were built as identical vessels at the port of San Blas, but they subsequently underwent changes in their structure and rigging at the port of Acapulco, located not far away. Each was a 45-ton vessel, 50 feet (14 m) long,[28] with a beam of 13 feet (3.7 m). They differed somewhat in their rigging; *Sutil* as a brig,

---

[28] The Spanish unit *pie* (foot) is about 11 inches, or 28 cm.

Mexicana as a schooner; however, in the reports of their voyage they are both called *goletas*, that is schooners.[29] Each had two brass guns, and was equipped with oars so that it could be rowed when necessary. These vessels were deficient in many ways, and Vancouver, who had ample opportunity to observe them, expressed the opinion that they were "in all the most ill-calculated and unfit vessels that could be imagined for such an expedition." Nevertheless, they had a light draft, were handy under sail and also when rowed, and Galiano was understood to state that "these vessels might be commodiously employed on difficult and distant excursions."[30]

Sutil would be commanded by Dionisio Alcalá Galiano, with Secundino Salamanca as second in command; *Mexicana* would be commanded by Cayetano Valdés, with Juan Vernacci as second in command. The expedition had no overall leader or commander but, with some justification, it has been called the Galiano Expedition.

Data

The main sources of information about the expedition are:
1) a concise early account signed jointly by Alcalá Galiano and Valdés; I call it *Extracto*, which is the first word of its title;
2) a long text, mostly written by Alcalá Galiano, which I call Galiano's report, narrative, or journal;
3) a similar report included in a book published in 1802 with a long title that begins with the word *Relación*. I shall use this word to identify it here;
4) drafts of 2) and 3), with variations from them;
5) notebooks.

Some of these texts contain errors, including one that has a bearing on the subject of this study.[31] None of the documentation records that Alcalá Galiano had some knowledge of English which turned out to be a very useful skill.

---

[29] A brig has at least one sail that is square-rigged, as opposed to the more modern-looking schooner-rig which has no yard. Charts drawn by the Galiano Expedition show as *Salida de las Goletas* (Schooners' Exit) the passage now named Goletas Channel on the northwest tip of Vancouver Island.

[30] Menzies' journal entry for June 26.

[31] The error is mentioned at the end of Chapter 7.

Some of the statements in these documents fail to draw a clear distinction between the Juan de Fuca Strait and the Strait of Georgia; that is, statements about one strait actually concern the other. These imprecisions have caused misunderstanding and errors in some publications.

English translations of *Extracto* and of all the relevant chapters of *Relación*, plus explanations, are included in Henry R. Wagner's book on the Juan de Fuca Strait. A translation of Alcalá Galiano's report, plus background information and many comments, appear in a book published by John Kendrick.

The expedition's findings in terms of coastlines, features and topography, are recorded in the charts that it produced, covering the whole of Vancouver Island, the Juan de Fuca Strait, and the Strait of Georgia. A number of first- and secondhand copies of these charts exist, with some slight differences in the shape of coastlines between various copies, and a few rather important differences in the toponyms used. In this work, for the sake of convenience, this cartography is referred to as the Galiano charts.

Stopover at Nootka; instructions for the exploration

On March 8, 1792, *Sutil* and *Mexicana* sailed from Acapulco and made directly for the Spanish establishment at Friendly Cove (Yuquot) in Nootka Sound, which they reached on May 13. There, the expedition spent about twenty-three days, during which changes were made to the ships' equipment and the composition of their crews.

The instructions they had been given by the viceroy included points that amount to the following:
- your main purpose must be a complete exploration of the Juan de Fuca Strait, and particularly "the determination of its northern and eastern limits";
- do not pay much attention to its "interior shores";
- chart harbours, bays, and islands;
- ascertain longitudes and latitudes, but with only a moderate accuracy, in the interests of "economizing time";
- if on the coast you examine you find indications of a navigable connection with the Atlantic, such as to the bays of Hudson and Baffin, and if your food supplies at the time are sufficient, you may navigate through this connection, all the way to Europe;

- if you actually make this navigation all the way, do not call at any "foreign port," unless forced by circumstances, in which case you must endeavour "by all imaginable means" not to reveal your findings to foreigners;
- however, since the existence of such an inter-oceanic connection is improbable, seek the route, suggested in Meares' book, from the Juan de Fuca Strait to the Queen Charlotte Islands, and thence explore the islands mentioned in that book;
- in any case, try to determine the coast between the Juan de Fuca Strait and Nootka [obviously implying the coast to the north of the Strait and around Vancouver Island].

These instructions were to the effect that they should continue the work of the Eliza expedition in the Strait of Georgia. Alcalá Galiano and Valdés probably had a copy of the aforementioned López de Haro chart of the Juan de Fuca Strait, and they certainly had a copy of the Eliza chart. At the time, Eliza, Narváez, Verdía, and other men who had participated in that exploration were at the Nootka establishment, and evidently had ample opportunity for briefing Alcalá Galiano on their experiences; however, there is no evidence that any such briefing took place, and the records of these two officers contain only a few rather vague references to the earlier expedition.

It would have been reasonable for Alcalá Galiano and Valdés to resume the Spanish explorations at the point where the Eliza chart left off; however, the chart included a feature that, evidently, aroused their curiosity. To the east of *Isla de Zepeda* and *Isla(s) de Lángara* there was the broad entrance, discussed above, which the Eliza chart called *Boca de Florida Blanca*, situated on what the chart suggested to be the continental shore at approximately 49°25'N. The written records of these two officers contain brief, but very emphatic statements, to the effect that they were eager to reconnoitre this *boca*, this mouth. While it seems that they considered it unlikely that this was the entrance to an inter-oceanic passage, they suspected that it might be the estuary of a major river.

When preparations were complete, *Sutil* and *Mexicana,* well-equipped with victuals and weaponry, had a complement of twenty-four men each, including the aforementioned commanders and seconds-in-command. Voyaging with the expedition was José Cardero, an amateur, but gifted young artist. The crews included at least one man who had participated in the Eliza expedition, and some men, including Valdés and Cardero, had been with the Malaspina expedition which had spent about two weeks at Nootka the previous year. One ship had "a gunner who was an excellent hunter." *Sutil* had two marine soldiers; *Mexicana* three soldiers from the "Catalan Company" which had been serving at Nootka. It appears that these three soldiers and some of the other men knew a little of the Nootkan language, and there is some evidence that commander Valdés did so too.[32] Each vessel had a sail boat that could either be carried on board when not in use, but no other craft. It is likely that the instruments they carried for navigation and for coastal surveying were of inferior quality to those carried by the Vancouver expedition. The equipment included articles such as copper sheets, axes, beads of various sorts, ornaments, hardware, and nails, for the purpose giving to Natives, either as presents or in barter.

Chapter 7 deals with this expedition's explorations.

---

[32]   While *Sutil* and *Mexicana* were at Acapulco, ten mariners who had been with the Malaspina Expedition, which had spent about two weeks at Nootka, were transferred to the two vessels.

A document in *Archivo General de la Nación* in Mexico City, Section Marina, Vol. 82, has particulars about the two vessels and about the equipment and personnel they had upon departure from Acapulco. Then, each had a crew of 20 men. The document contains information about changes in equipment and personnel that took place at Nootka, but there is no specific manifest on the matter at the time the *Sutil* and *Mexicana* departed for the exploration voyage. In any case, it should not be assumed that the crews were the same as when leaving Acapulco. The numbers in each vessel during the exploration voyage is reported in Vancouver's book: "twenty-four men bearing one lieutenant without a single inferior officer." The journal attributed to Bell (entry for June 13) says: "The Vessels were small, the Brig not being more than 45 tons Burthen (sic). They had each a Lieutenant, a Pilot, and twenty men and carried Two Brass Guns each." Since Vancouver was on board these ships several times, I rather trust his assessment than Bell's; this is why I assume the total number of the crew was 24 for each ship. Perhaps Bell's count did not include servants, or the artist José Cardero.

Chapter 6

VANCOUVER'S EXPLORATION

The Vancouver expedition arrived at Birch Bay on June 10, 1792, (June 11 by its own reckoning). *Discovery* and *Chatham*, with most of the personnel, in the charge of Commander Broughton, remained there, while two parties, using the ships' sail boats, reconnoitred in detail different parts of the coast of the Strait of Georgia and its inlets.

Vancouver had participated in the last expedition led by James Cook, which had spent about twenty-eight days at Nootka in 1778, but Vancouver gives no indication that he had learned any words of the Nuu-chah-nulth (Nootkan) language. Expedition members such as James Johnstone and Archibald Menzies, who also were with Cook at Nootka, may have learned a smattering of the Native tongue. Menzies had been at Nootka with the trader Colnett in 1787 and had spent time in the company of the Natives. The expedition also had copies of the books by Cook and Meares, which include lists of Nootkan words and expressions, along with their English translation.

Altogether, it is fair to assume that in conversations between Vancouver's personnel and the local inhabitants, each side spoke its own language, and communication was facilitated by facial and other gestures, and that some of the British did use a few Nootkan words. At one stage Puget commented in his journal, "The Ideas of these People could only be understood from the Expression of Countenance."

VANCOUVER-PUGET EXCURSION (June 11–22)

One of the two exploring parties that left Birch Bay was led by Vancouver and made use of two sail boats: a yawl or "pinnace,"[33] probably about 7.3 metres long, with a crew of about fourteen men including Vancouver, and a launch, probably between 5.5 and 6 metres long, with a crew of about ten men, including Thomas Manby and Peter Puget, who was the commander. The party was equipped with provisions for one week, a seine net for fishing, tents, weapons and ammunition, articles to give to Natives, etc. The areas reconnoitred include the one that is the subject of this study, and is shown in the respective fragments of the Baker and Vancouver charts printed as Plates 9 and 10.

Setting out from Birch Bay at 5:00 a.m. on June 11, the party proceeded northward. Around midday they reconnoitred the bays now called Semiahmoo Bay and Boundary Bay, "but the shoals attached to the shores of each, and particularly to those of the latter," prevented the group "from reaching within four or five miles [8 km] of their heads." Because of the shoals, the explorers were unable to get a very close view of the shoreline of the bays; nevertheless, they are depicted in the Baker-Vancouver charts much as they are known nowadays. Vancouver's book contains a brief description of them, but neither the expedition's written records nor its charts have names for them. Puget wrote that their inner southern point (Semiahmoo Spit) was "fine low level land and produced large quantities of tolerable flavored strawberries, and abundance of wild onions."

Observing the promontory marking the west side of Boundary Bay, Vancouver described it as "much elevated, at the south extremity of a very low narrow peninsula," and named it after Henry Roberts, who played an important part in the last of Cook's voyages. Menzies' journal refers to this feature as "a conspicuous White Bluff of a moderate height...which afterwards obtained the name Cape Roberts." In the Baker chart it is labelled Cape Roberts, in

---

[33] In his book, Vancouver refers to his boat as a yawl. Menzies' journal and the journal attributed to Edward Bell call it "the Pinnace." A yawl has one main mast and a smaller mizzen mast at the back; the small mizzen (sail) of a yawl extends out behind the rudder. "Pinnace" is from the French *pinasse*, meaning a small, two-masted, schooner-rigged ship's boat.

Vancouver's book and chart, Point Roberts,[34] which is now its official name. Puget's journal refers to it as "a white bluff," and reports an interesting event which must have happened early in the afternoon of that day.

> We stopped to dine at a deserted Village on the White Bluff. This must by its Size have formerly been the habitation of near four hundred People, but was now in perfect Ruins and overrun with Nettles and some Bushes, but as this Village differs materially from what we have already seen I shall notice what their construction appeared to be. The Body of the Village consists of two Rows of Houses, each Row divided by a Narrow Lane and partitioned off into four or Six Square houses and every one large and spacious. This frame, the only Remnant of the Village, must have [given] the Native inhabitants an infinite trouble in the construction and it still remains a Mystery to me by what powers of Machinism they have been able to lift up the heavy and long Logs of timber on top of Standards. The last are 2 1/2 feet [75 cm] in circumference and erected perpendicular about fourteen feet [4.3 m] from the Ground. On the Top of these Standards or Posts is a Notch cut to receive the Rafter, which from its length will serve for two houses or perhaps more, each Side and End of the house having three Standards to support it; Besides the Rafters going length ways, they are likewise laid across and with their Standards Partition off the Different Habitations. I have no Doubt that when occupied, the sides and Tops are boarded in, as large planks smoked dry were found contiguous to the village and if we could form an opinion from this Short and imperfect Visit it would be that the habitations are well adapted to defend the Natives from Inclement seasons.

Menzies' journal also contains some details of the village which, since he was not a member of the exploring party, he must have obtained from his fellow voyagers. His remarks include the following:

---

[34] Vancouver's book says, "which I distinguished by the name of Point Roberts." Menzies' journal entry for June 23 suggests that it was not precisely at this stage, but later, that Vancouver chose this designation.

...a large deserted village capable of containing at least 4 or 500 Inhabitants tho' it was now in perfect ruins...nothing but the skeletons of the houses remained.

Each house appear'd distinct and capacious, of the form of an oblong square and they were arranged in three separate rows of considerable length; the Beams consisted of huge long pieces of Timber placed in Notches on the top of supporters 14 feet [4.3 m] from the ground.... Three supporters stood at each end for the longitudinal beams, and an equal number were arranged on each side for the support of smaller beams in each house.

So, one can imagine the group led by Vancouver jumping ashore, leaving their two boats near the water's edge, carrying the wherewithal for lunch to the deserted village, having lunch, observing the ruins, commenting on them and wondering why the village was deserted. According to Baker's journal, he also sighted the ruins the following day from aboard the ship *Chatham*. These references make it clear that the village was situated close to the shore of Point Roberts, but they do not specify the exact location.[35] Perhaps the village had been deserted as a consequence of the devastating smallpox epidemic noted in Chapter 2.

From Point Roberts, roundabout, to Point Grey

Puget recorded: "We left the White Cliff about 1/4 past 2." That is, the group departed from Point Roberts at about 2:15 p.m.

Vancouver, observing the coast to the northward, noted particularly, "a low bluff point that seemed to form the southern entrance to an extensive sound." That is, he sighted the promontory to which he eventually gave its present name, Point Grey. The extensive sound was the kind of feature he was expected to reconnoitre in detail, and the group therefore with its two boats, proceeded in the direction of Point Grey. However, as Vancouver's book reports:

---

[35] John Work's journal says in an entry for December 20, 1824, "The point...is Vancouver's Pt. Roberts, part of the shore along which we passed is low clothed with grass and bushes and has a pleasing appearance. Towards the outer end the shore is bold and composed of clay with some rocks along the water's edge, at the very lower end is a low point of considerable extent entirely covered with an old Indian village."

[We] soon found our progress along the eastern or continental shore materially impeded by a shoal that extends from Point Roberts N80°W [280°] seven or eight miles [14 km], then stretched N35°W [325°] about five or six miles [10 km] further, where it takes a northerly direction towards the above low bluff point.[36]

The shoal was, of course, the extensive ground of alluvial deposits from the Fraser River, now officially known as Roberts Bank. Aware that the boats might run aground, the voyagers kept constantly sounding. Shallow water prevented them from keeping close to the shoreline between Point Roberts and Point Grey, and consequently, they were unable to survey it satisfactorily.

It was mid-June, a season of the year when in this part of the world visibility can be quite good until late evening. By about 9:00 p.m. it was still so good that the explorers could see land on the western side of the Strait. These were the islands now bearing the names of Galiano, Valdes, and Gabriola.[37] Vancouver estimated that at that time his party, in their two boats, were about half-way between the two sides of the Strait.[38] In the circumstances he led the boats toward land on the western side.

It is clear from the records that Vancouver's intentions were that: the group go ashore; a fire be lit; the members whose turn it was to be on night duty would cook food for the next day's meals; tents would be pitched; and the group would have some rest, but be ready to start moving again early the next morning. This was the usual procedure during excursions of this kind.

Fortunately, "the Night was fine and temperate," as mentioned in Puget's journal. The group reached the shores of one of the Gulf Islands, probably Gabriola Island, at 11:30 p.m. according to Puget's journal, but at about 1:00 a.m. the following day according to Vancouver's book.

---

[36] About 65 years later the British mariner Captain George Henry Richards, R.N. wrote: "Point Grey ... a long wooded promontory terminating in a rounded bluff is very conspicuous from the southward." (Richards, pp.108–113.)

[37] None of the three expeditions that explored the Strait of Georgia in 1791–92 (Eliza, Galiano, Vancouver) discovered that these Gulf Islands were not the eastern shore of Vancouver Island. The first European to discover this was Governor James Douglas in 1852.

[38] As Vancouver's book says, "...the shoal having forced us nearly into the middle of the gulph."

Unfortunately, the spot was unsuitable for making a camp. Thus recorded Puget, adding that the boats were anchored

> by the Side of a Barren and exposed Rock on which it was with difficulty we kindled a fire, nor could we find sufficient space for the tents. So we slept on [the] boats.

Vancouver's book says,

> ...it was with much difficulty we were enabled to land on the steep rugged rocks that compose the coast, for the purpose of cooking only, and were compelled, by this unfavourable circumstance, to remain and sleep in the boats.

Noon Breakfast Point = Point Grey

There is no information as to whether or not the group ate or drank something on that rocky shore during their stopover, which lasted only a few hours. They departed at about 5:00 a.m. the following morning, June 12, making directly for the eastern side of the Strait of Georgia, and, specifically, for that "low bluff point" they had sighted the previous day. Upon approaching it, they observed the shoals that spread out from the shoreline (Sturgeon Bank), which probably caused them to steer very carefully toward the shore.

Vancouver's book reports,

> ...we landed about noon, on the above-mentioned low bluff point which, in compliment to my friend George Grey of the navy, was called Point Grey.

However, it seems obvious that either Vancouver did not assign this name at that time, or else he did not inform Puget, whose journal records:

> We again visited the Shoals whose Edge we traced to a Bluff which for distinction's sake we shall call Noon Breakfast Point.

Why this appellation? As it seems that the expedition's records do not explain, a guess is in order. I assume that: the group had set out at an early hour having had no breakfast; that at about midday they had a hearty meal (the kind nowadays called "brunch") on the shore of that bluff; and that Puget, not knowing what name Vancouver would give it, designated it, provisionally, in commemoration of this late breakfast. As mentioned in Chapter 2, there are very good indications that in the late-eighteenth century there were streams of good drinking water, even in summer time, on the shores of Point Grey.

I assume that the British found such water and made use of it for washing themselves, making something to drink, replenishing their supplies, etc.

Exploring Burrard Inlet (June 12–13)

During the previous day, Vancouver, observing from the vicinity of Point Roberts the headlands that could be seen to the northeast, had formed the idea that they were the entrance to "an extensive sound." That is, his conjecture was that the inlets now called Burrard Inlet and Howe Sound constituted a single sound. Now he reiterated this notion and considered Burrard Inlet as the "southern" or the "eastern branch" of it. In his book this is designated as *Burrard's Channel*; in his chart as *Burrard's Canal*. Nowadays it is known as Burrard Inlet, but there does not seem to be precision as to whether or not the designation refers to the **whole** of the inlet between its entrance and Port Moody or just part of it. For the sake of convenience, in this work I occasionally designate as *Outer Burrard Inlet* that part west of First Narrows (edged by Point Grey, Point Atkinson, and Stanley Park); and as *Inner Burrard Inlet*, that part east of the Narrows (between Stanley Park and Port Moody.)

Vancouver and his companions proceeded to examine the inlet, starting probably in the early afternoon, by steering their boats into it. A comparison of modern charts with the charts produced by the expedition, and with statements in the records of Vancouver and Puget, reveals that these men formed the following notions:
- that the terrain of what is now Stanley Park was "a low rocky island producing some trees to which the name Passage Island was given";
- that to the north of this assumed island there was a rather narrow passage, what is now called First Narrows;
- that to the south of the supposed island there was "a similar passage ... with a smaller island before it," actually a narrow isthmus, now bounded by Lost Lagoon with False Creek to its south.

Contacts with Natives

Vancouver's group remained unaware that, twelve months earlier, the Spaniards Narváez and Verdía, navigating with a schooner and a longboat, had visited this part of the Strait of Georgia, though they had almost certainly not been inside Burrard Inlet. It is likely that on that occasion, Native people of the area had sighted the two vessels, and quite possible made contact with the Spaniards, and

69

that the two sides had engaged in barter. By the same token, it is possible that now, June 12, 1792, some Native inhabitants, sighting the yawl and the launch manned by Vancouver and his companions, came forth to meet them with expectations of barter. In any case, in the course of that day the explorers encountered Natives and bartered with them using articles from the stock that the group was carrying for that purpose. Vancouver's book and Puget's journal, which are the only sources information on the subject, differ very much with regards to the first encounters. The following are the detailed reports of the encounters:

(1)   Puget's journal, immediately after mentioning the group's arrival at the entrance of Outer Burrard Inlet, says:

> From Noon Breakfast Point the Continent takes a rounding Turn to the Eastward forming a very narrow Inlet with the opposite Shore. On its South Side is a Village from which we were visited by about 30 Indians, the Conduct of these People was friendly and inoffensive and from them we procured an Excellent Supply of Smelts in Exchange for Trinkets, etc. ... not a Weapon of any Sort were in the Canoes till asked for which they readily complied with, fetching these Articles from the Village, they trusted every thing in the Boats, with which they could hardly keep way, though nothing had been given in exchange for them.

The reference to weapons suggests that the British, wishing to obtain artifacts from this part of the world, asked the Natives to provide weapons such as bows, arrows, clubs, etc. in exchange for other articles, and that the Natives responded by going back to the village for the weapons and then tossed them into the British boats, trustfully, without prior agreement as to what articles they would receive in return.

(2)   Vancouver's book mentions that his party proceeded from Point Grey eastward and crossed the passage between that supposed island and the north shore, the First Narrows passage. So they were now in Inner Burrard Inlet. Following this note, the book states:

> Here we were met by about fifty Indians, in their canoes, who conducted themselves with the greatest decorum and civility, presenting us with several fish cooked, and undressed...resembling the smelt. These good people, finding we were inclined to make some

return for their hospitality, shewed much understanding in preferring iron to copper.

As mentioned below, Vancouver's book explains that these Native people came from "a small border of low marshy land on the northern shore intersected by several creeks of fresh water."

Vancouver understood that these people knew the difference between copper and iron. This detail and others in the data warrant the conclusion that these people had some native copper, but hardly any iron, and that they were eager to acquire objects or pieces of this metal.[39]

These statements are about the first contact of Puget and Vancouver with residents of the area of what is now the city of Vancouver and its vicinity. A careful reading reveals a considerable difference between what each man reported. Yet, it is assumed in some publications that both men referred to one and the same event and one and the same group of Natives. I doubt it very much, and <u>suggest these possibilities</u>:

- at the time, Puget and Vancouver were not navigating exactly in tandem but at some distance from one another; each traded in articles with a group of Natives, but with two different groups at two different places close to the entrance of the inlet;
- what Puget referred to as "a narrow inlet" was the First Narrows, between the north shore of Burrard Inlet and the terrain of what is now Stanley Park, on whose northeastern side was the village of *Whoi-Whoi*; about thirty of its inhabitants engaged in barter with Puget's group;
- Vancouver, from the yawl, met about fifty Natives who dwelt on the northern shore of the inlet, and he assumed that there was a village somewhere in that vicinity, although he could not see it. It may have been the *Homulchesun* village hidden by thick vegetation, near Capilano Creek.

From the vicinity of First Narrows, both British groups, leading their two boats eastward, reconnoitred its coast, while Natives in canoes followed them. The boats, being propelled by sails, could easily outdistance the canoes, but Vancouver, wishing to maintain the contact, arranged for the boats to move

---

[39] The Galiano Expedition which, a few days earlier, had been at Neah Bay and its vicinity, found that the Indigenous people had "bracelets of copper" and that for barter purposes they did not care for copper or for sea shells (mentioned in Museo Naval, Ms. 330). The Native people must have had a sufficiency of such decorative articles, or perhaps they had gone out-of-fashion.

slowly, "under an easy sail." Eventually the British reached the entrance to the arm of Burrard Inlet now called Indian Arm. They observed that there were two islets in front of the entrance and that, farther north, the arm was very narrow. From these observation they concluded that it could not possibly run far inland. Obviously, it was the kind of feature which by the instructions that regulated their voyage they should not bother to examine; "we had a grander object in contemplation," says Vancouver in his book. So, the party did not enter Indian Arm.

On two occasions the major part of the canoes pushed forward, assembled before the British boats, and the canoeists conferred among themselves. For a while the British were somewhat apprehensive about such "conferences," but the Natives never altered "their friendly disposition." It seems that occasionally the two sides communicated as best they could by sign language or mimicry. Vancouver wrote that the Natives manifested

> a great desire to imitate our actions.... They minutely attended to all of our transactions, and examined the colour of our skins with infinite curiosity. They did not have European commodities or trinkets except some rude ornaments apparently made from sheet copper.

From this and from their behaviour, the British commander assumed that these people had not had much contact with the Native people who traded with European or American ships. Most of the canoes "gradually dispersed," until only three or four accompanied the explorers, who then tried to fish by means of a seine net, but had "very little success." The Natives, having noticed this failure, led the British to understand that they planned to bring them "an abundance of fish" the following day. At some stage the voyagers, having decided to spend a night in the inlet, wanted the Natives to leave them alone, and tried to express this by means of sign language, but for a time the Natives remained and continued watching, with curiosity, the foreigners' moves and actions.

A case of the aforementioned desire to imitate occurred in connection with firearms. One of the foreigners fired a musket for some reason, perhaps aiming to kill a bird, as he obviously did not aim to harm the Natives. One of them expressed the desire to fire the weapon also. Permission was granted, and he did so, "though with much fear and trembling." Puget wrote:

> These People were wonderfully surprized both at the Report and Effect of a Musquet, they had waited in Anxious Expectation of one being fired and I have reason to think, it far exceeded, what their

Imagination had painted; they seemed to behold it with a Mixture of fear and admiration, and I think it not a little contributed to hasten their Departure, for they shortly after left us...we however contrived by Signs to convince each other of reciprocal Friendship.

Perhaps another factor contributed to their departure: the British gave them some presents of a nature not specified in the records.[40]

*****

It was about 6:00 p.m. when the Natives left the British, who subsequently went ashore at the spot just opposite Indian Arm; that is, at the location of present-day Barnet Beach Park.[41] There they made a fire, and probably had some dinner, perhaps eating what fish they had been able to catch themselves or what they had acquired from the Natives. They would have liked to sleep there, inside their tents, but the spot was "formed by steep rocky cliffs that afforded no convenient place for pitching the tents." Some of the men decided to sleep in the boats, but others, "for the sake of the fire...and without duly considering the line of high water mark," lay down on the rocky shore. They were in for a surprise. In the early morning they "found themselves incommoded by the flood tide, of which they were not apprised until they were nearly afloat." Indeed, "one of them slept so sound" that he might have been soaked and covered by water if he "had he not been awakened by his companions."[42]

*****

---

[40] Vancouver's book says that the Natives left "after receiving some acceptable articles." I do not like this expression, and lament that Vancouver did not specify what articles they were.

[41] Puget's journal, June 13 says, "Opposite to our Sleeping Place is a Small Branch, which I suppose terminates in our View, but its Narrowness would not be any prevention to its being examined, had we not been certain that it possibly could not run far." The "Small Branch" was undoubtedly Indian Arm and this detail reveals that it was on the beach opposite to it that the British went ashore.

Vancouver: "We landed for the night about half a league [2.8 km] from the head of the inlet, and about three leagues [17 km] from its entrance."

[42] "Early next Morning we were disturbed by the Tide floating through those who had preferred the beach for the sake of fire." So wrote Puget, who, on an earlier, similar occasion, wrote that this sleeping by the fire was done in order "to keep warm at least one side of the body." Although this happened in mid-June, the nights could have been quite cold in places such as the Barnet Beach.

At 4:00 a.m. that morning (June 13) Vancouver and his men started out in their two craft westward, back toward First Narrows. Vancouver's book contains the following paragraph in which I have underlined some phrases:

> As we passed the situation from whence the Indians had first visited us the preceding day, which is a small border of low marshy land on the northern shore, intersected by several creeks of fresh water, we were in expectation of their company, but were disappointed, owing to our travelling so soon in the morning. Most of their canoes were hauled up into the creeks, and two or three only of the Natives were seen straggling about on the beach. None of their habitations could be discovered, whence we concluded that their village was within the forest. Two canoes came off as we passed the island [the aforementioned supposed Passage Island, that is now Stanley Park] but our boats being under sail, with a fresh favorable breeze, I was not inclined to halt, and they almost immediately returned.

The first paragraph of this quote refers to the Natives that Vancouver's group had met the previous day, as reported above. It is the only reference contained in Vancouver's book about habitations in Burrard Inlet, and it suggests that he did not see any other village or camp within it.

Now for what Puget recorded about the Natives. His rough log says: "We had no visitors from the Tribe we passed yesterday." His subsequent log says, "We had no visitors from the villages we passed yesterday."

So, Vancouver's party with their two boats had now re-negotiated the First Narrows. Continuing their course westward, they reached the promontory now called Point Atkinson. It seems evident that it was not precisely at this time, but later, that Vancouver assigned the name Atkinson to the headland. His book explains that it is "situated north from Point Grey, about a league distant [5.5 km]," and that the party reached it at 7:00 a.m. Then, without mentioning any activity of the group, or anything further about the Native people, the book states that the group departed, northbound.

Puget's journal states:

> ...and [we] stopped to Breakfast opposite Noon Breakfast Point which bore due South about 3 Miles [5.5 km] to this place; the Indians were

---

In a general reference to this ten-day exploration cruise, Thomas Manby's journal says: "The nocturnal breezes blowing over frigid heights gave us many uncomfortable nights; as in our hours of rest the side next to the fire would be resting while the opposite would freeze."

not even enticed by our Smoke. Probably the Fire Arms kept them
away.

Surely, this reveals Vancouver and his companions went ashore on Point
Atkinson, made a fire for cooking and breakfasted. I surmise that when Puget
recorded this event in his journal, not knowing how to designate this place, he
did so merely by reference to the spot where the party had breakfasted at noon
the previous day, that is the shore at Point Grey.

*****

This stopover at Point Atkinson terminated the group's visit to Burrard Inlet,
which apparently lasted about eighteen or nineteen hours.

It is not recorded whether they actually reached the head of Burrard Inlet,
what is now Port Moody; however, the expedition's charts show this head fairly
accurately, and Vancouver's book says that the party, upon departing, was
perfectly satisfied with their exploration of the inlet. From this it is fair to
surmise that they reached close enough to its head to see that it was a waterlogged dead-end.

Whereas about other inlets or sounds of a similar kind Vancouver wrote
somewhat detailed descriptions, about this one he wrote only the above quoted
details and the following observations:

> The shores of this channel, which, after Sir Harry Burrard of the navy,
> I have distinguished by the name of Burrard's Channel, may be
> considered, on the southern side, of a moderate height, and though
> rocky, well covered with trees of large growth, principally of the pine
> tribe.[43] On the northern side, the rugged snowy barrier... rose very
> abruptly, and was only protected from the wash of the sea by a very
> narrow border of low land.

About the inner part of the inlet, Puget wrote:

> [it] extends 7 Miles [13 km] in a Straight Easterly Direction and in
> many Places only 1/4 of a Mile broad [0.5 km]. The North
> Shore...appears well inhabited and much broken by Small Rivulets.

---

[43] Although several species of pine grow in the Pacific Northwest, the western white pine
(*Pinus monticola*) and shore pine (*Pinus contorta* var. *contorta*) for example, most of the trees
seen here would have been Douglas fir (*Pseudotsuga menziesii*), red cedar (*Thuja plicata*), or
hemlock (*Tsuga heterophylla*). Vancouver, as did Menzies the botanist, applied the term "pine"
to every kind of coniferous tree.

Both Puget and Vancouver gained the impression that this was the first time that people from overseas visited this inlet. "I have no hesitation in venturing an opinion, that we are the Discoverers of this part of the Fuca Straights," says Puget's rough log.

George Goodman Hewett, surgeon mate, serving on the ship *Discovery*, collected artifacts acquired from Native peoples of parts visited by the expedition. Some such artifacts are now in the British Museum, London. Perhaps some are from this area.

Northward, and back to Point Grey

From Point Atkinson the expedition went on to reconnoitre Howe Sound, which, as mentioned, Vancouver considered to be the northern part of a very extensive sound; Burrard Inlet being its southern part. Then the British group proceeded to examine the coast to the north and northeast, including Jervis Inlet, whence, on June 20, they started their return trip to Birch Bay. So far, Vancouver had been navigating in the yawl, while Puget and Manby did so in the launch. However, at the time when both craft started moving, Puget happened to be in the yawl, while the rest of his group was in the launch, with Manby in command, at some distance away. The plan was for both craft to travel together, but, because of a misunderstanding, they became separated and did not meet again until after the yawl's arrival at Birch Bay.

Regarding the trip back by the yawl, with its own crew plus Puget, Puget's journal reports:[44] "that night we reached the Cluster of Islands in Mid Channel off Noon Breakfast Point." The latter was of course Point Grey. I imagine that the islands were perhaps the Winchelsea group (49°18'N, 124°05'W) at the entrance of Nanoose Harbour on Vancouver Island, or perhaps the nearby Ballenas group (49°20'N, 124°09'W) to the northeast and about two nautical miles [3.7 km] off the Vancouver Island coast, although neither group would be described today as being "off Point Grey," over thirty nautical miles away. In any case, it was in this area that Vancouver, Puget, and their companions spent the night of June 20 to 21. The following morning they had a surprise, which Puget's journal reports in these words:

---

[44] The return trip to Birch Bay of the launch commanded by Manby is reported in Chapter 8.

> We left our Quarters at 4 o'clock and soon after got sight of two
> Vessels under Noon Breakfast Point.

Vancouver's book, which makes no mention of the separation of the two craft, or of this stopover for the night, says:

> ...as we were rowing, on the morning of Friday the 22nd [June 21], for
> Point Grey, purposing there to land and breakfast, we discovered two
> vessels at anchor under the land.

At first Vancouver and his companions assumed that these vessels were *Discovery* and *Chatham*, but "on near approach," they observed that this was not so, and that the vessels were "wearing the colours of Spanish vessels at war"; that is, the official flag of the Spanish Royal Navy. They were, of course, *Sutil* and *Mexicana*, and Vancouver steered his yawl toward them.[45]

A report of this encounter is given in the next chapter, in the section titled "Encounter Alcalá Galiano-Vancouver."

---

[45] Quite accurately, both Puget and Vancouver referred to the *Sutil* as a brig and to the *Mexicana* as a schooner.

Chapter 7

ALCALA GALIANO'S EXPLORATION

On May 29, 1792, the Alcala Galiano expedition, with *Sutil* and *Mexicana*, and their sail boats, departed from Nootka and made directly for the bay that the Spaniards called *Núñez Gaona* (Neah Bay) at the entrance of Juan de Fuca Strait where another Spanish naval force was establishing an outpost with equipment, plants, victuals, domestic animals, including goats and sheep, etc., brought from Mexico. The expedition spent about two days at the bay, in the course of which it was provided with some fresh vegetables and perhaps also with a few goats. They also met local Natives, including a chief who, somehow overcoming the language barrier, managed to convey to them the information that there were two "English" ships inside the Strait.[46]

Leaving Neah Bay on June 8, *Sutil* and *Mexicana* proceeded along the strait and, two days later, made a stopover at Esquimalt Harbour, which the Spaniards called *Puerto de Córdova*. From there, the expedition moved eastward, anchored its ships off the southern tip of Lopez Island, then crossed what is now called Rosario Strait, and turned toward the continental shore, where they reconnoitred Bellingham Bay on June 11.

During the following day the expedition crossed the passage to the east of Lummi Island, and continued northward.

Late at night, as they were passing Birch Bay [which they called *Puerto Garzón*], from a distance, they saw lights, and assumed that the two ships they had heard about were there at anchor. Indeed, *Discovery* and *Chatham* were moored there, with most of their personnel; Captain Broughton was in charge,

---

[46] An expression in Galiano's report reveals that this chief was actually able to specify that the vessels were English.

and, earlier that day, some of them had sighted, at some distance, the two Spanish vessels, although they did not know their identity.[47]

Deception at Boundary Bay (June 13)

Now Alcalá Galiano and Valdés were eager to reconnoitre in detail the area which the Eliza chart [Narváez sketch] represented as an inner sea or basin that had, on its northwest side, a broad opening labelled *Boca de Florida Blanca*. The chart suggested that the vessels would be able to reach it from the south passing between *Punta de San Rafael* (Kwomais Point) and *Isla de Zepeda* (Point Roberts), or from the west through a passage marked by *Isla(s) de Lángara* (Point Grey) and *Punta de la Bodega* (the perceived north shore of Burrard Inlet, possibly Stanley Park).

The two Spanish ships continued sailing during the night of June 12–13, until Alcalá Galiano and Valdés reckoned that they were in the vicinity of the promontory that the Eliza chart showed as *Punta de San Rafael*. They spent the rest of the night tacking back and forth, holding their position. At dawn, they were able to scan the horizon and they concluded that the spot was, indeed, the bay flanked by *Punta de San Rafael* and *Isla de Zepeda*. Documents written by the Spanish commanders show that they were eager to find the large river, signs of which had been reported by their Spanish colleagues the previous summer.

A little later that morning, they began their search sending one of the expedition's boats ahead to check the depth of the water depth. At 5:00 a.m., *Sutil* and *Mexicana* started slowly moving in the same direction. At one time the boat was found to be in only one fathom of water (1.7 m).[48] The vessels had hardly moved one nautical mile (1.8 km) when they found themselves in water too shallow for safe navigation in the desired northward course. Consequently, as had been the case with Vancouver and his companions two days before, Galiano and his companions could not get close enough to the shore to examine it satisfactorily. Nevertheless, they could see that, where they

---

[47] At the time, Vancouver and Puget were exploring Burrard Inlet.

[48] A Castilian *braza* which is six Spanish feet (*pie*) or 1.68 m. An English fathom, also six feet, but English feet, is 1.83 m. A fathom is a very old unit of measurement approximately equivalent to the distance between the finger tips of outstretched arms, and it is unlikely to have been measured with a great deal of precision.

had expected to find that entrance to <u>a vast expanse of water</u>, there was a beach and, to the north of it, <u>a vast expanse of low land</u>, flat, swampy, "subject to flooding," and "full of trees." This was the modern-day Delta.

The expedition's miscellaneous notes include this statement about the *boca*:
> We found it all closed by a placer or mud [dirty sandbank] that left no channel and the boat in the middle found the bottom continually diminishing and we were very disappointed to see that from this side [southern] there was no possible entrance to the great River we had in view.

This, surely, is a strange statement. If accurate, it would mean that the Spaniards, from Boundary Bay, were able to sight the southernmost branch of the Fraser River, and this possibility appears to be nil. Perhaps, by "in view" the writer meant not literally in sight, but what he had in mind to find. In any case, there is no other such statement in the records.

The voyagers were able to see that what the Eliza chart showed as an island labelled *Isla de Zepeda*, was actually a small peninsula (Point Roberts). The expedition's records do not provide any additional details about the shape, features, and characteristics of this area and make no mention of the deserted village on the shore of Point Roberts described in the records of the Vancouver expedition. However, the chart produced by the Spaniards reveal that they gained a fairly accurate idea of the coastline. In the chart, the peninsula is labelled *Punta de Cepeda* [thus spelled], and Boundary Bay is labelled either *Bahía del Engaño* or *Ensenada del Engaño*. The words *Bahía* and *Ensenada* correspond to the notion of a bay or sound, respectively, and the word *engaño* means deception, or fraud. This designation evidently reflects the disappointment of the explorers upon finding reality sharply different from what they had been led to believe; that is, upon finding that there was no such feature as a <u>southern access</u> to the *Boca de Florida Blanca*.

They then decided to sail to the spot that the Eliza chart showed as *Isla(s) de Lángara* (Point Grey) and *Punta de la Bodega*, and as this seemed to offer another way to access the supposed *Boca*. Accordingly, *Sutil* and *Mexicana* started leaving Boundary Bay, headed for the entrance to Burrard Inlet. It was then that a British vessel was seen moving toward them.

Encounter with *Chatham*

Commander Broughton, knowing that during the previous day two vessels had sailed past Birch Bay, assumed that they were now somewhere to the north, and was anxious to contact them. So Broughton and other members of the British expedition, including the officer Joseph Baker, on board *Chatham* (which was provided with a boat, trailing astern), departed from Birch Bay at 4:00 a.m. on June 13.

About three hours later, this ship and *Sutil* and *Mexicana*, which were in the vicinity of Point Roberts, came within view of each other. At some stage each of the three ships displayed its national flag, ships and flags of two empires that had been at war with each other in the past, and would be again in the near future. However, for the moment there was peace, and each of the two expeditions was under orders from its government to act in a friendly and cooperative way with vessels and personnel of the other empire. *Chatham* neared the stern of *Sutil*, and it seems that the three vessels came to a standstill. Then, undoubtedly following standard procedure in such cases, and "with the utmost courtesy," the British asked the Spaniards' permission to send an officer to meet them. Permission being graciously granted, "a boat with an officer was sent on board the Brig [*Sutil*] where he was very politely received by the Commander"—so says the journal attributed to Edward Bell who was the clerk of *Chatham* and thus a secretary for Commander Broughton.

None of the records of this event specify in which language the British officer and the Spaniards communicated; however, as mentioned above, Alcalá Galiano had some knowledge of English. All the indications are that each man understood correctly enough what the other was saying. Each gave some information about his expedition, and declared that it would willingly assist the other if needed. The British officer suggested that the Spaniards move their ships to Birch Bay, where fresh water was available. The Spanish commander declined the offer on the grounds that at the time the winds were not favourable for the navigation this move would require, but they were favourable enough for continuing their northward exploration. Nevertheless, it seems that both men gained the impression that there would be further contact between the two expeditions.

One of the Spanish reports, and the book *Relación*, seem to state that it was Broughton who went aboard *Sutil*; however, none of the British reports supports this statement, and one of the manuscript notes from the Spanish expedition clearly implies that Broughton remained on board *Chatham* while one of its officers was on board *Sutil*. This manuscript, after mentioning the offer of help expressed by that British officer, says:

> ...we gave him due thanks and offered what was within our means by sending to the Commander some goat milk and the vegetables we still had from *Nuñez Gaona* (Neah Bay).[49]

Obviously, "we" means the Spaniards, and "the Commander" means that of *Chatham*, who remained on board.[50]

The journal attributed to Bell says:

> Don Galiano offered us every information and civility in his power and sent on board some milk and cabbages that he had brought from Nootka.

Surely, the cabbages and the milk were given in good condition for human consumption and this raises a question. It was sixteen days since *Sutil* and *Mexicana* had departed from Nootka, and six days since they had left Neah Bay. It appears that it was from this bay that the cabbages were taken aboard the ships and they were still fresh enough to be given to Broughton. But what about the goat's milk? Without refrigeration, there was no possibility of keeping it fresh for more than two days. How could the milk be fresh?

An event mentioned in Alcalá Galiano's narrative proves that on July 4 there were two goats on board *Sutil* and *Mexicana*, perhaps one on each vessel. From these facts it is fair to assume that these goats, and perhaps others, were on the ships at the time they departed from Neah Bay.

The boat that had brought the British officer to *Sutil*, returned to *Chatham*, which then proceeded to return to Birch Bay.

Galiano and his companions, with *Sutil* and *Mexicana*, left Boundary Bay, rounding Point Roberts, and by 2:00 p.m. they were off its western side in the Strait of Georgia heading for the entrance to Burrard Inlet, hoping to spend the following night there, and explore the inlet the next morning. However, things were not to work out that way.

---

[49] "...*hicimos los ofrecimientos que permitian nuestras facultades enviando al Comandante alguna leche de Cabra y las verduras que conservabamos de Núñez Gaona.*" Museo Naval.

[50] It is fair to assume that Broughton recorded the event in the journal he was keeping, but this document no longer exists.

Crossing Georgia Strait

What happened to them during the remainder of the day was much the same as had happened, two days earlier, to Vancouver and his crew who were sailing in the yawl and longboat. The Spaniards wished to sail northward, obviously intent on keeping sufficient proximity to the intervening coast to trace it carefully. However, after some time they found it hard going because the water was only two fathoms deep (3.4 m), which made navigation hazardous. They were clearly on the shoals now called Roberts Bank. This compelled them to "stand off" the coast; that is, to navigate at some distance from the shoreline.

At about 5:00 p.m. the Spaniards noticed that the colour of the surface water adjacent to the coast was turbid, and that current from that side was driving the vessels westward, toward the middle of the Strait. In view of this, some of the crew members "took to the oars," endeavouring to help the vessels to stem the current and advance to the north. However, the rowers, tired from similar exercise during the preceding days, failed to achieve that result. Consequently the Spaniards resolved to take "a course oblique to the current," and make for an anchorage somewhere on the western side of the Strait, where they saw land (the Canadian Gulf Islands, Galiano, Valdes, and Gabriola). *Sutil* and *Mexicana* reached the vicinity of one of them, probably Valdes Island, where they anchored in the late hours of that day, June 13.[51] During the subsequent two days they moved to another anchorage, on the northern coast of Gabriola Island, where they busied themselves, but also had some rest. For this reason they

---

[51] In relating these events, the outstanding and conscientious historian H.R. Wagner, in his book on the Spanish exploration of the Juan de Fuca Strait, made an error. In his summary of the *Sutil* and *Mexicana* voyage, his book contains a statement to the effect that they spent the night of June 13 at anchor on the eastern side of the Strait, "probably somewhere near the mouth of the Fraser River" and that the voyagers, wishing to have some rest, tried to find an appropriate anchorage on that side of the strait. The book then adds, "not finding any in the immediate vicinity, Galiano now took the strange course of proceeding to cross the Strait of Georgia to Porlier Pass." However, the book, (pp. 252–253) correctly translates into English what the book *Relación* reports about events in the course of that day (June 13), specifying that *Sutil* and *Mexicana* crossed the Strait of Georgia for the reasons explain here. That is, Wagner's own statement on one page of his book is erroneous, whereas another chapter of the same book correctly reports the events as mentioned in the book *Relación*. Wagner may not have been aware of the fact that Vancouver had crossed the strait two days before Galiano did, and for about the same reason.

called the anchorage *Cala del Descanso*, meaning Rest Cove, now officially named Descanso Bay. At some stage during the voyage they sighted inlets in which there were several abandoned villages. Perhaps yet further signs of the earlier smallpox epidemic.

Gabriola Island to Burrard Inlet (*Canal de Floridablanca*)

Leaving Descanso Bay at 5:00 a.m. on June 19, the Spaniards re-crossed the Strait of Georgia, making for the area that the Eliza chart (Narváez sketch) showed as a broad entrance between *Isla(s) de Lángara* and *Punta de la Bodega*, which they had failed to reach six days before. The sailing was erratic, and the trip took the whole of that day.

Sutil had an anchor hanging on its starboard side, and was towing its boat. A crew member was on watch on the ship's bow, but at some stage he failed to detect danger, as, at about 9:30 p.m. the ship collided with a thick, large, and dry tree, visible by its branches, which was floating with the current. The tree got entangled with the ship's anchor and for some time there was "considerable danger" that it would hit the boat. However, reacting opportunely, the Spaniards managed to free the anchor, and the boat remained undamaged.[52] By midnight they found themselves at a spot very near a stretch of coast characterized by "low land," and they decided to spend the rest of the night standing on and off.

AT POINT GREY AND BURRARD INLET

Events of June 20

In the early hours of June 20, with the benefit of daylight, the voyagers considered themselves to be at the spot which in the Eliza chart was labelled *Isla(s) de Lángara*. They referred to it by this denomination in some of their

---

[52] Galiano's journal places this incident at 9:30 a.m., adds that two similar trees, looking like rocks awash, were sighted six days earlier, and guesses that such trees "came out" from the body of water that the expedition's records at that stage begin to call *Canal de Floridablanca*, that is, Burrard Inlet.

manuscript drafts and notes. Eventually, however, (these records do not specify how and when) the voyagers must have realized that there was no island, but instead an extensive headland. Then, correcting the designation from "island(s)" to "point," they named this terrain *Punta de Lángara* (Point Grey).

It seems likely that during the rest of that morning Alcalá Galiano and Valdés sighted enough of the western side of Burrard Inlet to conclude that it was erroneously drawn in the Eliza chart, and to suspect that it was inaccurate in respect to the opening it showed, labelled *Boca de Florida Blanca*. In any case, some of the expedition's records, reporting the early events of this day, apply to the whole of Burrard Inlet the designation *Canal de Floridablanca* (correctly spelled) as being in honour of Count Floridablanca. Now Galiano and his companions assumed that there must be a major river estuary inside this "Canal," this inlet.

If only because the Eliza chart so indicated, and perhaps also from talking with Narváez, the two Spanish commanders knew that there were shoals bordering the shore of *Punta de Lángara*.[53] Accordingly, they took the normal precautionary measure of sounding when approaching land. At one time they found that the water depth was 40 fathoms (67 m) and, fifteen minutes later, only 3 fathoms (5 m).[54] Later on, noticing that the wind was blowing from the west, the water level was decreasing, and the current was pushing the vessels toward the shore, the voyagers dropped anchor in order to wait for better conditions. The spot was probably at a short distance to the southwest of Point Grey (see Appendix 2).

Nine days earlier, the yawl and the launch manned by Vancouver, Puget, and their companions had arrived at this inlet, and bartered with the Natives. Perhaps news of this appearance of strangers spread among the local communities and the news contributed to the fact that, now, local Native people in canoes, evidently prepared for barter, came forth to meet the Spaniards, who

---

[53] The expedition's records have some comments about the misconception formed by Narváez and Verdía about this area and its topography.

[54] At this stage *Relación* says, "we know from information of other voyagers and from our own experience that one could suddenly pass from very deep to very shallow waters." Much the same statement appears in Galiano's report. Neither document specifies who were those other voyagers, but they could be Narváez and Verdía, whom Galiano met at Nootka.

were navigating with two vessels, larger and more impressive than the yawl and the launch.

First contact with the Natives

The first contact occurred early that morning (June 20).

Seven medium sized canoes, very similar in shape to those seen at the entrance of the Juan de Fuca Strait, came from the SSW of *Punta de Lángara* (Point Grey) and made for the schooners. The voyagers, as European naval officers were required to do, carefully recorded their observations of the Natives, and included the following details:

- each canoe carried two or three Indians, whose faces were "painted red," but with the colour somewhat faded. Most of them, having taken off their capes or cloaks, were stark naked. Some wore hats in the shape of truncated cones, and some wore necklaces of nacre (mother-of-pearl);
- physically, the people were of medium height, with longer eyes, less flat noses, darker skin, better-shaped features, and faces "more perfect" than those of the other Indians seen in the channel [probably meaning the Strait of Georgia]. Their muscles were less "full," but were better shaped than those of the Nootkans;
- they were lively, talented, and spirited, with indications of a warlike disposition. Some youngsters in the group spoke with wit, and some resembled the youngsters of "Mulgrave Bay" (the present-day Yakutat Bay, in Alaska, which Cayetano Valdés and Juan Vernacci had visited the previous year);
- their language was like that of the inhabitants of Wenthuysen Bay (the region of Nanaimo Bay, on the eastern coast of Vancouver Island);
- articles they carried in their canoes included: blankets like those of the Wenthuysen Bay people, boxes and baskets for carrying fishing gear, stone harpoons, spearheads, clubs and pikes about half a yard[55] long [42 cm] with tips of either iron or flint, quivers with bows and with arrows that had the same kind of tips, and rope or line made of seaweed.

---

[55] A *vara* (yard) was three Spanish feet, about 0.84 m. An English yard is 0.91 m.

One of these men presented the Spaniards with a salmon, evidently without expecting anything in return. A confusing statement in the records suggests the following:

- the Natives were given beads which they accepted without showing appreciation;
- they were offered knives and shells, perhaps suggesting barter, but they showed no interest in the articles;
- when requested to barter one of their clubs, they refused because what was offered in return did not satisfy them.

This encounter between the Spaniards and the party in the seven canoes was soon over. The canoes then departed.[56] It was probably while this encounter was taking place, and while *Sutil* and *Mexicana* were at anchor, that a current was "running out," tending to push them far away from the coast. The crews, raising anchor, set them on a SSW course.

Second contact with Natives

Eventually the vessels were anchored, provisionally again, at a spot estimated to be at some distance to the SSW of *Punta de Lángara* (Point Grey).

There, at about 9:00 a.m., four canoes moved toward the vessels. Three of the canoes were small, of the same size as those the voyagers had seen earlier, and each carried three people. The fourth canoe was larger, and carried six people, including two boys who were paddling and an old man of conspicuous seriousness who was wearing a hat which indicated he was a chief. Invited to come on board *Sutil*, he did so immediately, "showing frankness and confidence."

The Spaniards presented the people with beads but the recipients did not seem to care much for them, "preferring iron and copper." At some stage a deal was made; the Natives provided the foreigners with "a small canoe" in exchange for two small copper sheets weighing five or six Spanish pounds each (approximately 2.5 kg). However, the bargain did not include paddles for the canoe.[57]

---

[56] This encounter is mentioned in the book *Relación* but not in Galiano's report.

[57] The records do not agree on this detail but I go by the one that says that paddles were acquired later as mentioned below.

The records specify that this party, with four canoes, had come "from the southern part of *Punta de Lángara*." A manuscript draft of Galiano's report has two marginal notes, omitted in the final text. One note says that after this encounter the Natives departed, making toward the middle part of the coast between *Lángara* and *Cepeda* Points (between Points Grey and Roberts). The other note says that the canoes "withdrew to the *Punta de Lángara* where there was a village."[58] There is discrepancy between the two notes, but the second one provides evidence of a Native village in this area.

Anchoring off Point Grey

Shortly after this encounter, the voyagers made anchor at a spot where the surface water was "almost fresh," and logs were seen floating by. These observations the voyagers took to signify that there was indeed a major river estuary inside *Canal de Floridablanca* (Burrard Inlet). Around midday of June 20, the two vessels moved to a point off of Point Grey, which was probably about the same place where Narváez had anchored the *Santa Saturnina* and its companion longboat about eleven months earlier, as indicated by the sign of an anchor in the Narváez sketch.

Third contact with Natives

After *Sutil* and *Mexicana* were had anchored, the following events took place:
> In the afternoon, twelve Canoes came close to us with some Natives who treated us with friendly countenances and signs of confidence. Their language seemed very similar to that of the Indians we saw in *Descanso Cove*, but they are of a nobler soul and disposition. One of them came on board,[59] and was combed and decorated with a ribbon;

---

[58] These notes are:
• *"Los Indios se retiraron dirigiendose azia la costa por la mediania entre las puntas de Langara y Cepeda."*
• *"Se retiraron las Canoas a la Punta de Langara donde havia una rancheria."* This second note is crossed out in the manuscript, perhaps because the other one was more correct, but it is a very important note in that it reveals the existence of that village.

[59] On board one of the vessels, probably *Sutil*.

he was very pleased with this, and gave many embraces to the man who had so adorned him. They would repeat with great facility whatever we were saying to them. We sang the song Malbourgh [or Malbrough]. The Indians, once they picked up the tune, joined in the singing and continued singing it by themselves even after we had finished. They sold us some bows, arrows, clubs, and also three paddles for the canoe, as the Indians from whom we had acquired it had departed without equipping it [with paddles]. None of them was to be seen in the afternoon, and, consequently, we were certain that they were not from the village that we saw near *Punta de Lángara* [Point Grey]. They had repeatedly made signs to us that we should go towards the interior of the Channel, inviting us there with much to eat and an abundance of water.[60]

The context of this passage warrants the conclusion "the Channel" was *Canal de Floridablanca* (Burrard Inlet). Thanks to this encounter with the Natives, the Spaniards now had paddles for the canoe.

What is known about the song?

At least two books in English, published in recent times, affirm that the song was one titled *Marabú*, which originated in Andalucía, Spain. I have solid reasons to feel sure that it was not this song, but one which was well known in some countries of Western Europe, and also in Mexico. It was sung in different languages at that time in history, and even much later. Its melody is similar to, some people say the same as, that of the popular English song "For he's a jolly good fellow." Its title was spelled and pronounced in different ways, depending on the country: Mambrou, Malbroug, Malbrough, Mambrú, Mambrut, Malbrú, Malbourg, Malbruk, etc. Some publications contain assumptions or assertions about the song's origin. One of them is that it was related to the exploits of the famous British general the Duke of Marlborough (1650-1722). The Spanish version of the song begins with the line, *"Mambrú se fue a la guerra...."* In 1790 and 1791, that is, before the events studied here, personnel then serving at the Spanish establishment at Nootka, sang that tune with a few words in the local language, some Nuu-chah-nulth people learned it, and there is evidence that they enjoyed singing it too.

---

[60] This passage is a close rendering of what Galiano's report and the book *Relación* mention about this encounter.

One of the expedition's manuscripts has a brief report about these contacts of June 20, which is significant in these respects:

- it has a marginal note saying that these people's "dress" did not differ from that of the Nootkan people;
- it has another such note in these words *les cambiamos flechas, macanas y fisgas*, which I take to mean that, by barter with the Natives, the members of the expedition acquired arrows, clubs, and fishing harpoons;
- it states that in the afternoon the Natives returned, "although without their women and lads."

The last assertion implies that the Native groups met in the morning included some women and lads. I have not found any other reference of this kind in the expedition's records, which, on the whole, may give the impression that the Spaniards did not see any women or children in the vicinity of Point Grey.

Puget's journal states, retrospectively, that in the course of that day Galiano had "run the Launch going away to the southeast," but gives no details. This suggests that Galiano had taken a trip with one of the Spanish launches to the southeast of Point Grey, but I have not found any reference to such move in the Spanish records. If it actually occurred, what could have been the purpose? Examining the coast to the south of Point Grey? Contacting Natives of the area? In any case, if Galiano had gone far enough south, and got relatively close to the shoreline, he would have "discovered" the north arm of the Fraser River, and the event would have been recorded, but he either did not see or did not notice that feature.

In human terms, the main events of that day were the three contacts with local people in canoes: seven canoes with two or three Natives in each; four canoes with perhaps a dozen persons altogether; and another twelve canoes. This makes a total of twenty-three canoes, and probably over sixty Natives, that came to *Sutil* and *Mexicana* on the waters in the vicinity of Point Grey. This is more canoes and more people than the Vancouver-Puget group had come across nine days before.

In this connection the records reveal that the explorers were astonished at the difference in face, build, and character, but not their clothes, between Natives of different communities in the general region of the Juan de Fuca Strait and the Strait of Georgia. These differences existed even between groups living within a few kilometres (leagues) of one another.

The expedition, with its two ships and three small craft, remained at anchor southwest of Point Grey during the subsequent night (June 20–21). Perhaps it was a clear night, as, at 2:00 a.m., somebody noticed that a massive log was being propelled by the current toward the prow of *Sutil*. The ship's crew, with appropriate handling of the helm and of an oar, were able to prevent a collision of log and ship. I imagine that this event in the middle of the night must have caused everyone aboard some loss of sleep.

June 21 - Encounter Alcalá Galiano-Vancouver

At 7:00 a.m. the next day, the Spaniards saw a boat coming their way. It turned out to be the yawl in which Vancouver, Puget, and some of their companions were travelling toward Birch Bay, but which was making a stop for breakfast at Point Grey. The boat was brought alongside *Sutil*. Then Vancouver, Puget, and one of the midshipmen[61] in their group went aboard this ship, where they were welcomed by Alcalá Galiano and his crew. Thus took place a meeting of English-speaking and Spanish-speaking men; the kind of meeting that could be handicapped by a language barrier.

None of the three British officers spoke Spanish. How was the language barrier overcome? The matter is not mentioned at all in the Spanish records. However, Vancouver's book says that Galiano "spoke a little English"; while Puget's journal asserts that the Spanish commander "spoke English with great Ease and Fluency." These are quite differing perceptions about the man's proficiency, but revealing enough. It is on the basis of these statements that I mention elsewhere in this work that Alcalá Galiano had some knowledge of the English language.[62] Surely, it was thanks to this fact that the language barrier was overcome during this meeting of the Spaniards and the British.

---

[61] Probably the midshipman Robert Barrie according to J.E. Roberts. Galiano noted that the same midshipman accompanied Vancouver when they met on Kinghorn Island.

[62] As implied above, Galiano's own report about this voyage does not mention this very important fact. Nor is it mentioned in the book *Relación* which, until very recent times, was practically the only publication with a detailed report about the voyage of *Sutil* and *Mexicana*. Any alert reader of the book, when coming upon the pertinent passage about the encounter between the two Expeditions, would wonder how the language barrier was bridged. Readers of the Spanish reports would have no explanation (such was my case for a very long time). Readers of Vancouver's book would find its reference to Galiano's moderate knowledge of English. Puget's journal remained unpublished and virtually unknown for nearly 200 years; so it had few readers.

Perhaps, when the three visitors arrived, the Spaniards aboard the *Sutil* were about to have breakfast. In any case Vancouver's book records that he partook with them "a very hearty breakfast," but fails to mention whether Puget and the midshipman partook as well. Menzies' journal clearly implies that they did.[63]

*****

Surely the rest of the British group, perhaps about eight in number, must have had breakfast as well, but nothing about it is mentioned in the records; thus it is fitting to express suppositions.

This is the kind of situation which writers of history fiction can enjoy depicting according to their fancy. It could be done in one way or the other depending on what the writer considers to be the personalities of Vancouver and Galiano. For instance, this way:

Where did these subordinates of Vancouver have their breakfast? On board the yawl? This would have been cumbersome, and it is fair to assume that it did not happen. On board *Mexicana*, courtesy of the Spaniards? Perhaps...but perhaps at another place, known to them, and by a sequence of events, as follows.

While Vancouver, Puget and the midshipman who accompanied them were climbing aboard *Sutil* and greeting the Spanish officers, the rest of the British remained on the yawl, waiting for instructions from their commander. On the decks of the two vessels and in their boats, were many Spaniards looking at the British. After a while, Vancouver and Galiano, having reached agreement on one point, stood on the deck of *Sutil*, and ordered a call for silence. Then, facing the British yawl and their occupants, Vancouver addressed them in these terms:

"This gentleman beside me is Captain Galiano of the Spanish Navy, and he has kindly invited the three of us here to breakfast with him and some of his officers. I suggest you go to where we had that memorable noon breakfast nine days ago, have an early breakfast, and then load some fresh water on the yawl. By the way, you may take the food and drink that was to be for the three of us."

Then Captain Galiano, in moderately good English, shouted words to this effect: "Very cordial greetings to you, British young men. I suggest you

---

[63] "They went on board the Brig [*Sutil*] and were politely detained for breakfast," says Menzies' journal, pp. 62-63.

meet some of the Spanish ones, and have a cheerful time together." Then looking at the rank and file Spaniards, he shouted, "*y vosostros, jóvenes españoles, id a abrazar a esos británicos y a pasar un rato feliz con ellos.*" Thereupon the British on the yawl moved toward the spot near a spring where they had had that noon breakfast. A number of Spaniards, using one or two of their boats and the wherewithal for breakfast, made the same move. So, here were two groups of young mariners, all very far away from their respective home places, eating, drinking, and enjoying each other's company. They belonged to two rival empires, but each group was full of empathy with the other. They were handicapped by a language barrier, but each side addressed the other with expressions of goodwill in its own language, aided by mimicry and gesticulation. Expressions like these were uttered, "*Somos amigos.*" "It's nice to meet you, Spaniards." "*Viva Inglaterra!*" "We like Spanish wine." Questions were asked about navigation; about family, but probably misunderstood; questions about girlfriends, with gesticulations, perhaps understood. They exchanged gifts of tobacco and biscuits; the Spaniards treated the British to wine. At about 8:40 a.m., a Spanish officer, conveyed in the canoe obtained from local Natives, arrived to tell the two groups to return to the anchorage of *Sutil* and *Mexicana*, and this was done.

So much for conjecture!

*****

Regarding what was spoken, suggested and agreed upon between the Spaniards and the three British aboard *Sutil*, it is fair to assume that each side wanted to abide by the orders it had been given to act in a friendly way toward the other side. Their respective records do not quite tally with each other on details, but agree in asserting that the meeting was very friendly and that each side provided information about itself, its aims, and recent experiences. Concerning matters that have a bearing on the subject of this work, the following points are clear enough:

- each side was displeased to find that the other side, representing a rival empire, was engaged in exploration of that part of the world;
- each side reported to the other on what parts of the Juan Fuca Strait and the Strait of Georgia it had covered and charted;
- the Spaniards examined the "sketch" of the explorations Vancouver had made in the region of Burrard Inlet, Howe Sound, and Jervis Inlet, and took from the sketch "such notes as they pleased," says Vancouver's book;

- Vancouver mentioned that "the only spot" of Burrard Inlet that he "conceived" to have left unexamined was the arm situated on the northern side, that is the one now called Indian Arm;
- Alcalá Galiano told Vancouver something of the exploration Narváez had made in that area, including some reference to an opening named *Boca de Florida Blanca* (or *Floridablanca*), and about the belief that somewhere, perhaps through this opening, a copious river flowed into the sea;
- Vancouver specified that he had not found any river of consequence in the whole of Burrard Inlet, and that it reached only 14 miles [26 km] to the east of Point Grey;
- Vancouver's book states that Alcalá Galiano and his companions "seemed much surprised that we had not found a river to exist in the region we had been exploring, and named by one of their officers *Río Blancho* in compliment to the then prime minister of Spain which these gentlemen had sought thus far to no purpose."

From what is reported in the previous pages it is perfectly justifiable to assume that Alcalá Galiano did <u>not</u> say that a Spanish officer had assigned to that supposed river the appellation *Río Blancho*.[64] Obviously, and perhaps because of Alcalá Galiano's deficiency in spoken English, the British captain did not quite understand what the Spaniard stated. In any case, the Spaniard learned that Vancouver had not found any river of consequence in the whole of the area he had reconnoitred, including, Burrard Inlet.

More or less explicitly, the two sides agreed to join efforts in exploration of the parts of Strait of Georgia they had not yet covered. Each would incorporate into its cartography parts that it had not covered by copying from the cartography of the other expedition.

Changing plans

Alcalá Galiano and his companions had arrived at the vicinity of Point Grey intent on proceeding, with *Sutil* and *Mexicana*, to reconnoitre the inlet that they had begun to call *Canal de Floridablanca* and check whether, perhaps at its head, there was the supposed mouth (*Boca de Florida Blanca*) shown in the

---

[64] There are very good reasons to assert, as I do, that Galiano might have said *Río Floridablanca*, but certainly not *Río Blancho*.

Eliza chart. Now, after conversing with Vancouver and seeing, and perhaps copying, the sketch he had drawn of this inlet (Burrard), they had to conclude, once and for all, that there was no such mouth, no such river. However, there is some inconsistency in the expedition's records in that in some places they refer to the inlet as *Rio de Floridablanca*, even after this encounter with Vancouver.

As a result of that meeting aboard *Sutil*, the Spaniards were willing to forego reconnoitring the inlet, and were envisaging the possibility that they and the British would move to Birch Bay. However, the weather was a factor to bear in mind. Vancouver considered the wind was favourable enough for navigation of his yawl, and, having already spent on his ongoing excursion much more time than he had planned, he was anxious to leave as soon as possible for Birch Bay.

The Spaniards considered the wind not favourable enough for navigating *Sutil* and *Mexicana* and consequently made new plans. With the benefit of what they had learned from Vancouver they would examine Burrard Inlet, including Indian Arm, which he had not examined. Perhaps for good reasons, they apparently thought that it would be wise not to use for this purpose *Sutil* and *Mexicana*. For the time being both vessels would remain at anchor, as well as the canoe obtained from the Natives, while some of their personnel would undertake that exploration with the launch and boat, and return to that spot. It was agreed that in due course the Spanish expedition would move from Point Grey toward Birch Bay and meet the British expedition there, or perhaps the two expeditions would meet mid-way.

Vancouver was told that if his sailors were very tired from the rowing the yawl, as they had been doing lately, he could be provided with Spanish sailors as rowers for his return to Birch Bay, but he declined the offer. So he and all of his companions stepped into the yawl and departed from Point Grey at about 9:00 a.m.[65]

Shortly thereafter, a group of Spaniards, with their launch and boat, departed from the vicinity of Point Grey to examine the shorelines of Burrard Inlet, after

---

[65] Galiano's report implies that he suggested that Vancouver and his men could return to Birch Bay transported by *Sutil* and *Mexicana*. It may have been an early offer subsequently changed by the offer to provide sailors from those ships to help row the yawl. Puget's journal says, "We left the *Soutile* [sic] about nine".

having made arrangements for a rendezvous in case that upon returning they found the two schooners had departed.

Sutil and *Mexicana*, the aforementioned canoe, and a number of Spaniards, probably twenty-eight, remained on board ship anchored off Point Grey. For various reasons it would have been risky to attempt the manoeuvre of getting the two vessels close enough to the shore so that these men could easily step ashore; for purposes such as this one and other vessels of this kind were provided with smaller craft. At this stage the only craft they had was the canoe.

The records do not specify that the canoe was used, but it must have been, for some purpose or other, as they state that at some stage during that day it was found to leak badly from a crack in its bottom, that the personnel took it aboard one of the ships to be repaired, and that, probably because the task was proving too difficult, they asked for help from the Natives. One of them came aboard and directed the repair, which was done very successfully.

This is the only activity the records mention for the rest of that day, but they mention that observation of the tides in the area gave the impression that their movements had no regularity or pattern with regard to direction of time of the day.

So much for events near Point Grey on June 21, 1792.

*****

During the next day, the Spaniards continued having some contact with the Natives. Probably with implicit reference to the brig *Sutil*, one document says approximately the following:

> This morning we had alongside, for a short time, one canoe only; in the afternoon there came four, the Indians being with the best harmony, but despite this we did not cease being watchful, paying special attention astern [the ship], where they had always come close, with their canoes, and put their hands through the cabin windows. However, we could not consider them thieves, not even after a sailor missed a pair of pants he was drying together with other linen which the abundance of sweet water had enabled the sailors to wash. This disappearance was noticed and that sailor expressed it with some signs that the Indians understood immediately; standing up, they shook their blankets and mats, demonstrating that none of them had stolen the pants.

Galiano's report states that, aiming to prove their innocence, the Natives also took off the cloaks they were wearing. Another document tells these events in almost the same terms but instead of sweet (fresh) water, says <u>brackish water</u> (*agua salobre*). This information does not reveal whether or not they eventually found the pants, but reveals that the Natives of this area had mats, and that some of the Spanish sailors washed their linen with local water.

This washing raises questions such as: Was the water really fresh, or merely brackish? Where was the washing done? Where were the clothes dried? Where were the Natives who maintained that they did not steal the pants? etc.

If the water was brackish, that is, on the sea level, chances are that some was taken aboard, emptied into basins, and clothes were washed there and hung on ropes held along the sides of *Sutil*, or *Mexicana*, or both vessels.

If the water was really sweet, the washing was probably done at some stream or pond ashore, the clothing laid out on rocks or bushes to dry in the sun, and that there were some Natives in the vicinity.

Surely, there is glow in the idea that some Spaniards went ashore to have breakfast with the British, and that the next day some Spaniards returned to the spot to wash their clothes and stretch their legs.

On the subject of further contact between strangers and local inhabitants during that day, one report states:

> They continued behaving most cheerfully and we did likewise in all our actions. We sang them the Malbrough, and each of them joined in the chorus; they, too, kept time, not only with the tune but also with hand-clapping and other motions of head and arms. Afterwards they treated us with a song of their style, keeping the rhythm by striking their canoes with their paddles and with other sticks, and pausing for half a second between strokes.

The Spaniards found this song somewhat similar to what in their language is called *canto llano*, which is similar to Gregorian chants.[66] Subsequently, the Natives sang a different tune in which they repeated a word that in the records is spelled *alesié*. [In figurative English spelling it could be *ah-lay-sea-ay*.] In addition to the Malbrough, Mambroug or Mambrú, the Spaniards sang other songs in their language, and the Natives picked them up with much interest and desire to pronounce the words correctly. By way of presents, these people were

---

[66] *Canto llano*: Medieval style of church music (liturgical chant) still used in the rituals of the Roman Catholic Church. It is monodic and rhythmically free. The expression is also applied to traditional melodies of the same type. The English equivalent is plainsong.

given some beads. At nightfall they departed from the schooners' side, very pleased, continuing to sing their songs and those they had just learned.

Later in the night the Spaniards heard "many voices" and "much shouting" ashore, from which they assumed that the Native people continued to sing their tunes. The Spaniards continued on watch, with weapons at the ready, just in case they were wrong. Perhaps these Natives resided at the small village or summer camp that appears to have existed on the site of Point Grey.

*****

With respect to the party that had gone to reconnoitre Burrard Inlet, the records suggest the following. Alcalá Galiano and Valdés, on the basis of what they had learned about the inlet from conversations with Vancouver and from the plan of it which he showed them, assumed that the party would return to Point Grey on June 22; this not being so, the two officers began to worry, and even considered going to search for them, but decided to wait until the following day. At dawn that day (June 23), they watched, perhaps with the help of a telescope, for a glimpse of the launch and boat. These were not to be seen at the time, but they later came to view at 5:30 a.m., probably as they emerged from the passage now known as "First Narrows." Half an hour later they arrived at the schooners' side.

EXPLORATION OF BURRARD INLET
(*Canal de Floridablanca*)

Now for details about that exploration of Burrard Inlet, which the expedition's records refer to as *Canal de Floridablanca*. The task was effected by a crew commanded by the officer Juan Vernacci with the *Sutil's* launch, and another group led by the officer Secundino Salamanca with the *Mexicana's* boat, probably about twenty men altogether. They took along some articles for the purpose of giving them to the Natives, either as presents or in barter. There is a hint that they carried a copy of Vancouver's sketch of the inlet. In any case, it is evident that these men charted its shores, including those of Indian Arm.[67]

---

[67] What seems to be the only existing firsthand information about this exploration appears in two short accounts among the expedition's notebooks (in Naval Ms. 144). These accounts do not bear their authors' names and are written in the first person singular and/or plural, which I

*****

This excursion lasted about forty-one hours, including two nights, but the records say nothing about where and how the party spent the nights, or about any stopover for meals. The following is an account which incorporates nearly all the information, and adds comments.

At 11.30 a.m. on June 21, the launch and boat set out from the spot where they and their ships had been moored, near Point Grey. It appears that, at least part of the time, the wind followed the trend of the tides, the boats could sail together, and navigation was fairly easy.

By 4:00 p.m. the two craft were at the basin ("lagoon," says one account) that forms the head of the inlet (that is, in the area of the present-day Port Moody) and, the only part that remained to be examined was what their records call "the northern arm of the Canal," that is, Indian Arm.

During the rest of the time this arm was explored right to its head, plus the lower part of the rivulet that empties there. However, the accounts do not mention when this was done. Given the length of this arm, it must have taken several hours to cover it both ways. In view of this I consider it very likely that the voyagers spent the first night somewhere near the head of Burrard Inlet, and most of the second day reconnoitring Indian Arm.

The following are, largely in the same terms as in the existing data, the somewhat-confusing details mentioned about the area:

Regarding Burrard Inlet in general:

It has steep shores, many of which are rocky; others are mountains of considerable height. There are thick stands of close-spaced tall coniferous trees[68] and impenetrable underbrush, many streams of sweet water and some waterfalls produced by melting snow that whitens the crest of a mountain range that can be seen from the ravines. The mild temperature, the lushness of the different shades of

---

consider proof that the authors were participants in the trip: probably its two leaders. These accounts say nothing specific about the outer part of Burrard Inlet; about its inner part they say very little, except for Indian Arm, on which they provide a few details. Partly because these passages do not appear in any other publication, either in the original Spanish or in English translation, they are transcribed in the Appendixes of this work.

[68] One of the manuscripts says pine trees. The Spanish tended to apply the term "pine" to all conifers, as did the British.

green, the multitude of wild rosebuds and some meadows with fruits such as blackberries, gooseberries, and currants, make of this place a delightful abode that in many parts of Europe would prodigiously combine utility, ease and splendour.

Regarding Indian Arm:

This arm is about 16 miles [30 km] long and ends in a river of sweet water that is narrow and of little depth, runs down the slopes and gorges of a high mountain, and is navigable only a short distance.[69] We entered it, navigating in half a fathom of water [0.8 m], and the boats were exposed to being dashed to pieces against the trees of the banks. The trees and debris accumulated there impeded further penetration of the boats along the rivulet.... This part has a forest where we saw some huts, and some Indians in their vicinity.

This description may be compared with the following one, resulting from an exploration of this arm effected, sixty-five years later, by the British mariner, Captain George Henry Richards, R.N.:

North Arm...runs in a general northerly direction for 11 miles [20 km]. It is entirely different in its character from other portions of the Inlet [Burrard Inlet]...it is enclosed on both sides by rugged mountains raising from 2,000 to 5,000 feet [600 to 1500 m] almost perpendicularly and down the steep sides of which the melting snow in summer forces its way in foaming cascades rendering the surface water with the inlet below all but fresh.

The head terminates in a delta in swampy rushes, through which some rapid streams find their way into the inlet from a deep and narrow gorge in a NW direction.[70]

This gorge where rapid streams flow must be what the Spanish report calls "a river of sweet water and of little depth." It is now called Indian River.

*****

---

[69] Subsequently, Vancouver learned from the Spaniards that this arm was "very narrow, leading in a northern direction nearly three leagues [17 km]."

[70] Richards, *Vancouver Island Pilot*, pp. 108-113.

As for contacts between the participants in this exploration of Burrard Inlet and its inhabitants, Alcalá Galiano's journal and the book *Relación* contain some information. The same information, plus additional details appear in two brief reports about that exploration. One report says: No Indians were seen from shortly after the time when the boats left the schooners until they reached

...the mouth of the sweet water river [at the head of Indian Arm], where there were many Indians, in villages. Our appearance in our two boats alarmed the women, and their menfolk hid them in the bushes. We treated the men with courtesy and presents, while at the same time taking steps not to be surprised by them; they watched carefully our doings and left us very soon!

The other report is written in the first person singular, which clearly suggests its author was either Vernacci or Salamanca. It contains the following passage:

In the Channel that we call *Floridablanca* and the Natives call *Sasamat*, there are few inhabitants. At the entrance I have seen two villages [*rancherías*]. Several of their Indians brought their canoes alongside our boats, they presented us with fish and expressed satisfaction in meeting us. Their garments, weapons, etc., were very similar in every way to those of the Indians we had met earlier, but I did not find them to be as robust and skilful as those we had seen coming from the vicinity of *Isla de Cepeda* [Point Roberts].

Comment: The two villages may have been *Eyalmu* and *Homulchesun*, but they may have been *Whoi-Whoi* close to False Narrows and *Snauq* along by the entrance to False Creek.

That account goes on to state:

We saw no other Indians during our navigation along the eastern arm [I guess, meaning the length of Inner Burrard Inlet], but when we finished our navigation of the North Arm [Indian Arm], we saw, on the banks of the river in which that arm ends, a small village from which the women immediately fled as soon as they saw us. Some of the men embarked in their canoes and came closer to us, especially a young man who seemed to be the *tayee* [that is, the Chief][71] who was giving orders and was obeyed by the Indians in a way that we had not noticed in other parts. They were more clothed, with capes, than the

---

[71] The word for chief is spelled in different ways both in the Spanish and English records.

Natives of the entrance to the Inlet, but both groups had the same kind of blankets. After spending about one hour with us, these Indians of the North Arm went further into the river, jumped to land and, carrying their weapons, went into the woods.

Since José Cardero was in the Galiano expedition for the specific purpose of drawing sketches, he might have participated in this exploration, sketched that village at the head of Indian Arm, and made a portrait of that young chief. Alas, there is no evidence whatsoever that such was the case.

*****

It was undoubtedly from this excursion and from what observations they made otherwise, that the Spaniards formed an idea of the shape of the whole inlet and incorporated the information in their charts. These reveal that the Spanish group viewed the terrain of Stanley Park as constituting an island, as it had been so perceived by Vancouver and Puget.

Sasamat - original name for Burrard Inlet?

Without explaining how, where, and when they acquired the information, the expedition's records state that the Natives of the inlet called it *Sasamat*. It would seem that these people uttered a word or expression that the explorers, correctly or not, understood to be the place name, and wrote it down on the basis of Spanish spelling. Spelled phonetically, it would be *Sæsamæt*. An approximation to English spelling could be: Sah-sah-maht. As mentioned below, the inlet is so named in one of the published Spanish charts of the Galiano expedition. From the location of the name in this chart, and from its mention in the records, I conclude that the Spaniards assumed it applied to the whole of the inlet, not to Indian Arm only as stated or implied in some publications. (See item *Sasamat* in Appendix 4.)

Miscellanea

While exploring, the Galiano expedition collected pieces of wood, specimens of plants, as well as artifacts from the Natives. For instance, one manuscript says, in reference to arrangements for the exploration of Burrard inlet, that it was expected that the participants would collect wood of different kinds, plants, and other things, to add to the expedition's collection.[72]

Some acquisitions of Native artifacts are mentioned above. A still-existing list of articles acquired in the course of the voyage specifies those obtained at "Langara Islands," which evidently means the area around Point Grey. The articles are: three very good clubs, one harpoon, one canoe, and three paddles.[73]

The expedition's records include a few statements about the nature of the territories and inhabitants of Nootka, Clayoquot Sound, the Juan de Fuca Strait, the Strait of Georgia, and makes some comparisons.[74] Some characteristics or details might have been common to the whole region. The records[75] also mention that, somewhere in the area of the Strait of Georgia, there were dogs of medium size, similar to English dogs, mostly white and very furry, and that most of them had been sheared and the wool put to good use.

Departure from Point Grey

Two hours after the return of the exploring party, that is, at 8:00 a.m. on June 23, the whole expedition departed from the vicinity of Point Grey. *Sutil*

---

[72]   Museo Naval, Ms. 144, fol. 444.

[73]   "*tres macanas, mui buenas, una fisga, una Canoa, 3 canaletes en Is. de Langara.*" Museo Naval, Ms. 330, fol. 74.

[74]   In its account of this exploration of Burrard Inlet, the book *Relación* includes a digression that might seem to be inspired by observations made in the inlet, but which does not fit precisely its characteristics. Consequently, I suggest it be considered to refer, in general, to the various inlets the Spaniards visited on the intricate coast of the Juan de Fuca and Georgia Straits. The digression includes passages such as these:

> ...arms of the sea, usually tortuous...formed by the sides of very high and steep mountains...clad with pines and crowned with snow, which, when it melts, forms most lovely cascades...copious rivers in which breed a quantity of salmon...inhabitants who know how to provide themselves with sustenance, satisfy their needs and protect themselves from their enemies.... The visitor entering these channels may perhaps think he has found the desired communication with the other sea [the Atlantic], or an easy access to the interior of the continent, but he is disappointed in finding, on turning a bend, that the mountains of the two sides close, forming a narrow beach....

[75]   Museo Naval, Ms. 144, Cuaderno 2, fol. 494. See Kendrick's *The Voyage of Sutil and Mexicana*.

and *Mexicana* had spent about sixty-six hours there. Two of the expedition's manuscripts and the book *Relación* have an error that implies that the stay lasted two days longer.[76]

---

[76] Galiano's report in Museo Naval [Ms. 619], one in the Mexican National Archives [*Historia* 55, fol. 152], and the book *Relación* state that the date of departure was June 25. If true, this would mean that the Expedition stayed in the area an extra two days, but, as neither the book nor the manuscripts report any activity for such days, the reader might wonder whether the Spaniards really did nothing. The date is obviously a mistake, as proved by other documents that report departure as occurring on June 23, which tallies perfectly with data from the Vancouver Expedition. The dating baffled me for years until I discovered this evidence of error.

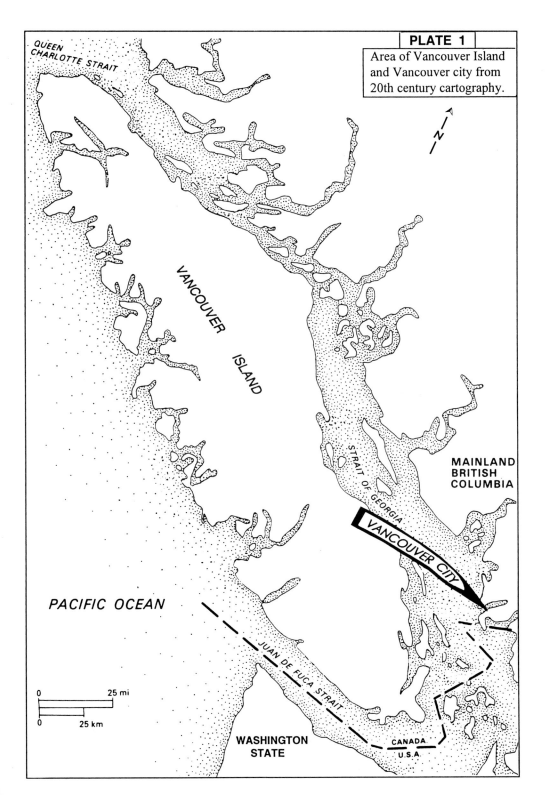

PLATE 1

Area of Vancouver Island
and Vancouver city from
20th century cartography.

QUEEN
CHARLOTTE STRAIT

VANCOUVER

ISLAND

STRAIT OF GEORGIA

MAINLAND
BRITISH
COLUMBIA

VANCOUVER CITY

PACIFIC OCEAN

JUAN DE FUCA STRAIT

0   25 mi

0   25 km

WASHINGTON
STATE

CANADA
U.S.A.

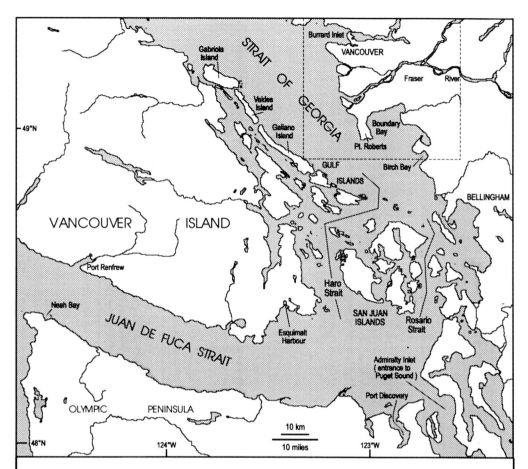

The southern approaches to the Vancouver area (marked by the rectangle, top right)

Access to Vancouver from the North Pacific Ocean is via the Juan de Fuca Strait, through the San Juan Islands, and into the Strait of Georgia, a journey of about 250 km (160 miles). Vancouver Island, which has drifted to its present position from far out in the Pacific over geological time, is hilly and forested at its southern end. Across the strait in Washington are the snow-clad peaks of the Olympic Mountains.

The San Juan and Gulf Islands, which are also geologically distinct from the rest of the region, obstruct the flow of water between the two straits, and strong tidal flows among the islands are common. Haro Strait, which leads into Boundary Pass, marks the border between Canada to the west and the USA.

The whole area was once densely populated with aboriginal communities.

PLATE 2

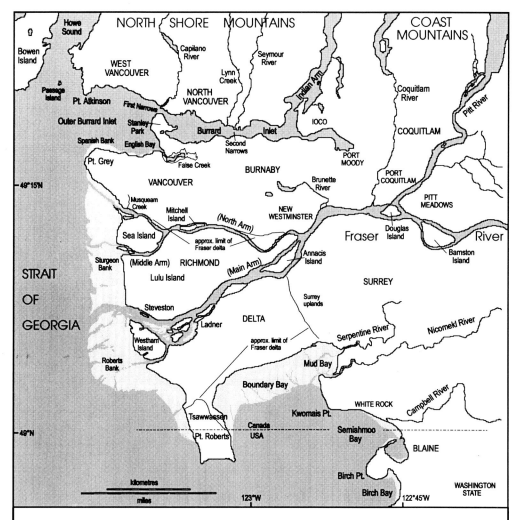

A modern map of Vancouver and the surrounding lower mainland area

To the north are the Coast Mountains (known locally as the North Shore Mountains). Howe Sound, Burrard Inlet, and Indian Arm are partially-submerged valleys, typical of the B.C. coast. Vancouver, Burnaby, Surrey, White Rock, and Pt. Roberts are situated on layers of glacial till, sand, clay, and gravel dating from the last ice age and earlier. This gently-rolling landscape, once heavily forested, is commonly a few hundred feet above sea level. Richmond, and Delta sit on recent river deposits protected by dikes and dredging, and for the most part only a few feet above the sea. This land did not exist 10,000 years ago, and Pt. Roberts was once an island. The Fraser River continues to build its delta along the edges of the tidal flats of Sturgeon and Roberts Banks.

False Creek has been extensively filled in historical times (shown on the map by the thin line) and Lost Lagoon in Stanley Park was formerly an inlet. Note that this book identifies the parts of Burrard Inlet to the east and west of First Narrows as "inner" and "outer" Burrard Inlet respectively.

PLATE 3

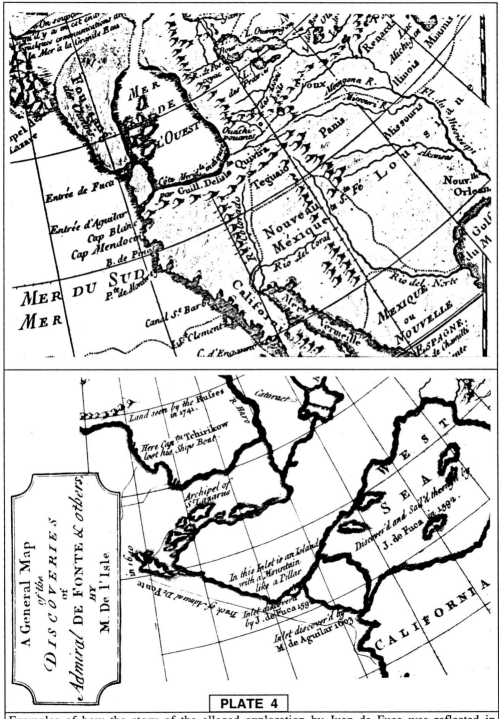

PLATE 4

Examples of how the story of the alleged exploration by Juan de Fuca was reflected in maps printed in France and England circa 1754.

Haywards Straits

Sea Otters Sound

Sketch of the Track of the

Port Meares

NORTHERN ARCHIPELAGO

Sketch of the Track of the American Sloop Walhington in the Autumn of 1789

THE SEA

Land Seen

THE SEA

55°

Bucclugh's Sound

Stephens Sound

PRINCESS

ROYAL

ISLANDS

North I.

Douglas Entrance

Q. CHARLOTTES

Banks I.

ISLES

Gibsons I.

C. S.t James

Calverts I.

C. Scott

Fitzhugh's Sound

NOOTKA or King Geo Sound

50°

Berkleys Sound

John de Fuca's Straits

M.t Olympius

Shoal Water. Bay

A CHART
of the Interior Part of
NORTH AMERICA
DEMONSTRATING the very great probability
of an
INLAND NAVIGATION
from HUDSONS BAY
to the
WEST COAST

PLATE 5

Title and part of a map in the book by John Meares, published in London in 1790. It shows the western coast of Vancouver Island. The representation of the space to the east of the island and of the track of the sloop *Washington* are imaginary. The degrees of latitude, as inscribed elsewhere on the map, are added here.

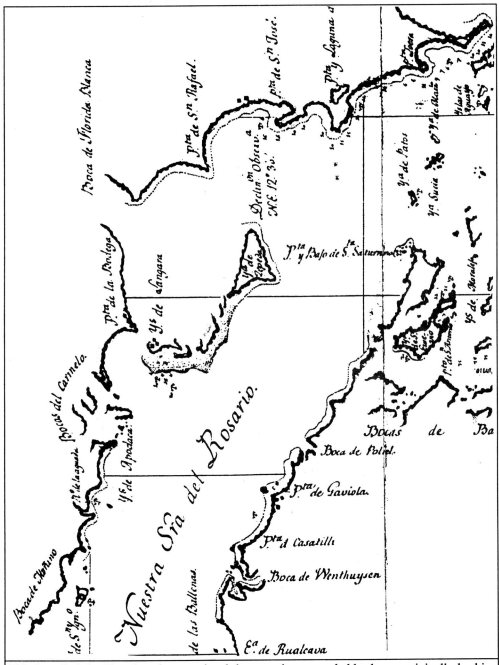

Boca de Florida Blanca

Pta de Sn Rafael.

Pta de Sn Josse.

Pta y Laguna d

Decln. Observa
NE 12° 3o.

Yta de Zepeda

Pta la Bodega

Ys de Langara

Pta y Bajo de S. Saturnino

Ys de Haralds

Bocas del Carmelo

P. de la laguna

Ys de Apodaca

Boas   de   Ba

Boca de Poliel.

Nuestra Sra del Rosario.

Pta de Gaviola

Pta d Casatilla

Boca de Wenthuysen

Boca de Florino

de Sn Igno

de las Ballenas

Ea de Rualcava

Yta de Patos

Ya Suria   Ya de Maia

Ysla de Aguayo

Pta de Sann

This is called the Narváez chart or sketch because it was probably drawn originally by him from his surveys of the area and subsequently incorporated into the map (called Eliza map) on which were reflected the findings and explorations carried out by the expedition led by Francisco de Eliza in 1791. It reveals how Narváez envisaged (and misunderstood) the water and land corresponding to the site of Vancouver city and its neighbourhood. See also Plate 7.

PLATE 6

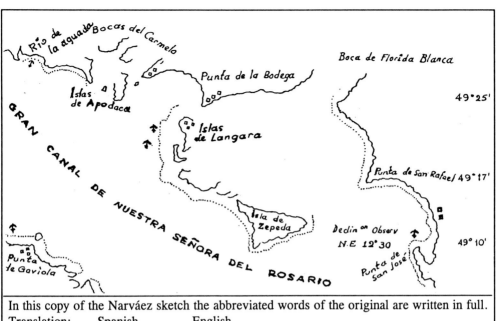

In this copy of the Narváez sketch the abbreviated words of the original are written in full.

Translation:

Spanish	English
Río	river
Isla, islas	island, islands
Punta	point, headland
Boca, bocas	mouth, mouths (entrance to rivers, inlets or channels)

Note anchors in three places.

| PLATE 7 |

Conjectured configuration of the hull of the schooner *Santa Saturnina*, based on principal dimensions recorded by José Maria Narváez in 1791.

Numbered hull components are:
1. captain's deck
2. quarterdeck
3. main deck.

From a thesis on Spanish vessels by Malcolm Hall Kenyon (1965).

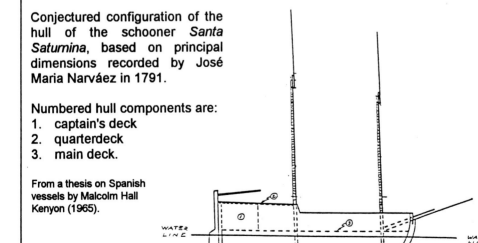

| PLATE 8 |

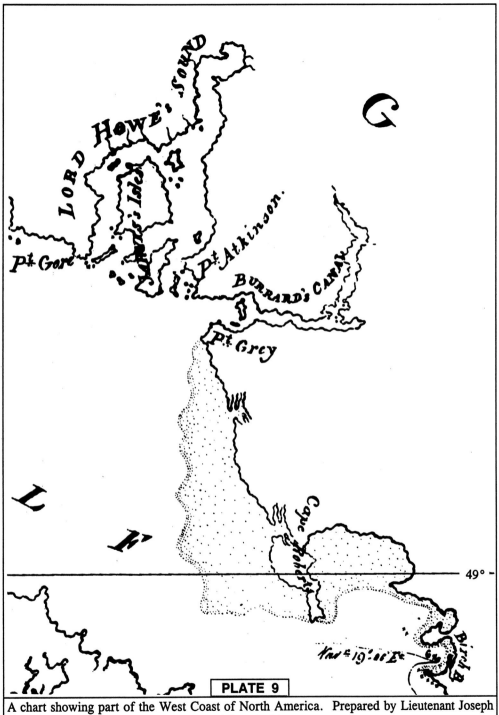

G

LORD HOWE'S SOUND

Pt Gore

Pt Atkinson

BURRARD'S CANAL

Pt Grey

L

F

Cape Roberts

49°

Birch B

Nov 19. 11 E.

PLATE 9

A chart showing part of the West Coast of North America. Prepared by Lieutenant Joseph Baker under the immediate inspection of Captain Vancouver.

Courtesy of the Hydrographic Department of the British Ministry of Defense.

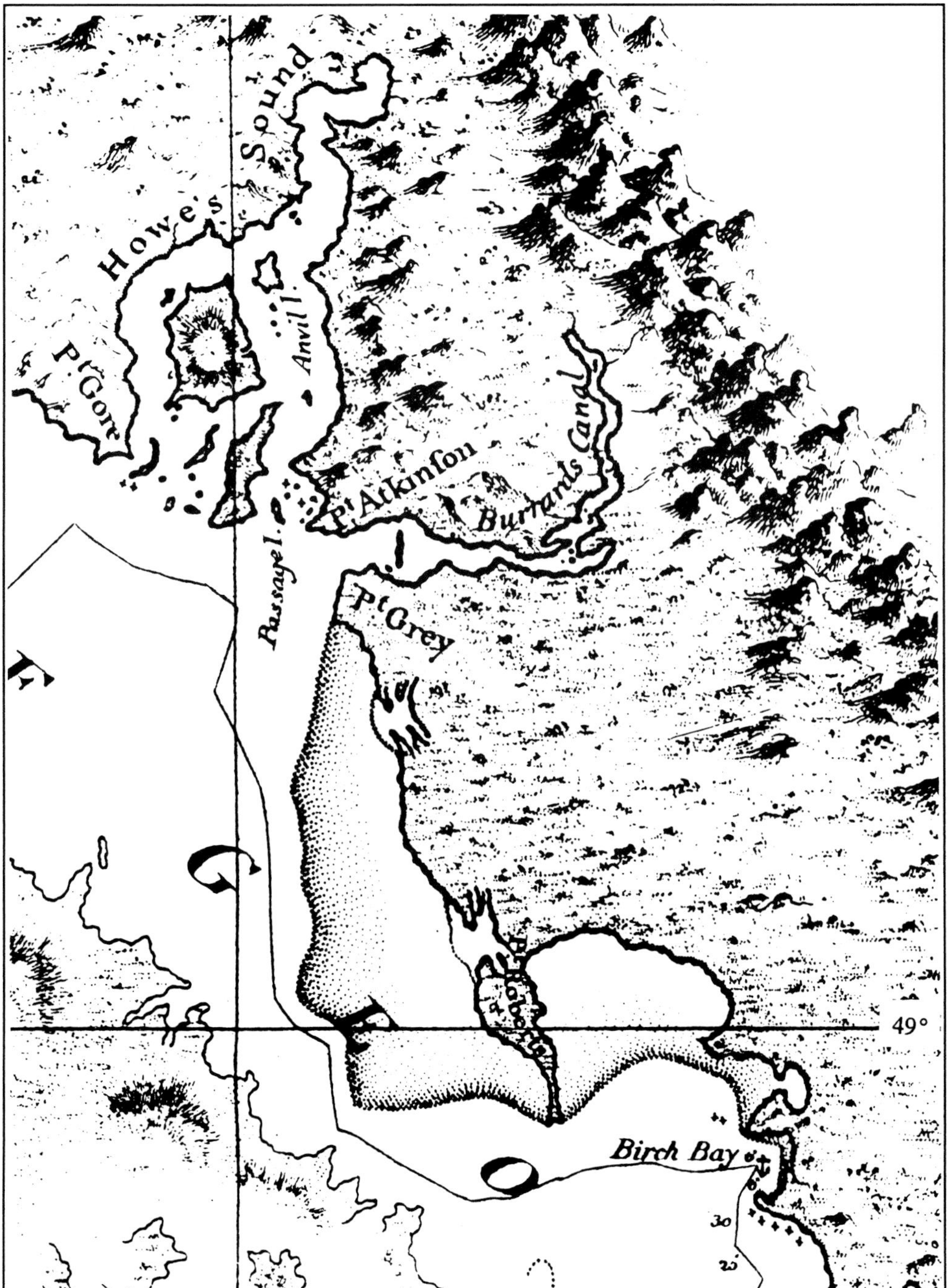
Howe's Sound
Anvil I.
P.t Gore
P.t Atkinson
Burrards Canal
Passage I.
P.t Grey
Birch Bay
49°
30
20
PLATE 10

The part of Baker's chart shown on the opposite page as it appears in the *Vancouver Atlas* published in 1798. The peninsula of Point Roberts is badly copied from Baker's chart.

THE COAST OF THE AREA OF VANCOUVER CITY AND ITS VICINITY AS SHOWN IN MAPS DRAWN BY THE ALCALA GALIANO EXPEDITION. (See Chapter 8, Section OVERVIEW.)

In the following three maps the dotted lines flanking shorelines represent areas of shores or banks.

Galiano Map 1: The zone in a manuscript map drawn in 1792, but not printed. Burrard Inlet is called *Canal de Florida Blanca*.

Galiano Map 2: The earliest printed representation of this zone. Portion of a map printed in Spain in 1795. In it Burrard Inlet is labelled *Brazo de Florida Blanca*.

Galiano Map 3: The same part in a map included in the atlas companion of a book about the Galiano Expedition, published in 1802. In this map Burrard Inlet is labelled *Canal de Sasamat*. (See Appendices 3 and 4.)

Other place names in the maps:	Their official names:
Ensenada del Garzon	Birch Bay
Ensenada del Engaño	Boundary Bay
Punta Cepeda	Point Roberts
Punta de Langara	Point Grey
Brazo del Carmelo	Howe Sound
Bocas del Carmelo	Howe Sound
CANAL DEL ROSARIO	GEORGIA STRAIT
Cala del Descanso	Descanso Bay (N.E. tip of Galiano Island)

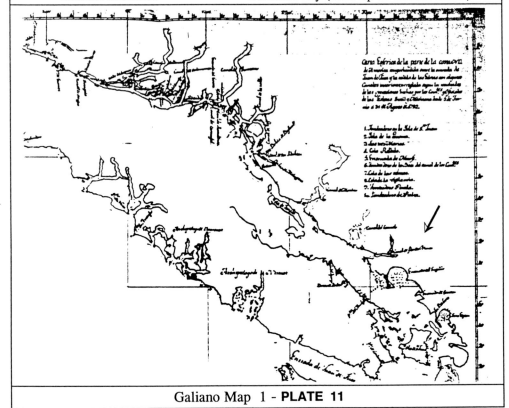

Galiano Map 1 - **PLATE 11**

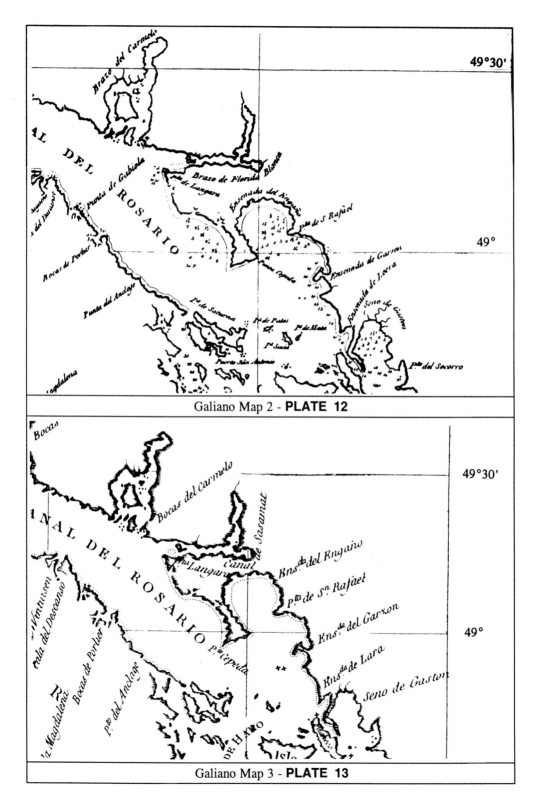

Galiano Map 2 - **PLATE 12**

Galiano Map 3 - **PLATE 13**

BOATS OF THE VANCOUVER EXPEDITION

The Vancouver Expedition carried two cutters, two launches and one yawl. Lieutenant Commander Andrew David, formerly attached to the Hydrographic Office, British Ministry of Defense, Taunton, England, explains: "A yawl appears to be a smaller boat than a cutter and equipped with perhaps six to eight oars. It would probably be manned by six to eight oarsmen, a coxswain and two officers. It may seem unusual that Vancouver would have chosen the smaller boat for his explorations but perhaps the yawl was designated as the captain's boat and that he used in preference to the cutter in spite of the fact that it would be smaller and perhaps a little more cramped. The launch would appear to be a little larger than the cutter."

PLATE 14

Part of a drawing by John Sykes of the Vancouver expedition. It shows a cutter, probably drawn in Port Townsend on the southern shore of Juan de Fuca Strait.

One of the Galiano Expedition's boats and some native canoes in what is now called Loughborough Inlet, to the north of Georgia Strait (not the zone of Vancouver city!). From an original drawing by José Cardero, "improved" by other artists.

PLATE 15

PLATE 16

VESSELS of the ALCALA GALIANO EXPEDITION drawn by José Cardero. Courtesy of Museo Naval, Madrid. *Sutil* and *Mexicana* (officially designated *goletas*, i.e. schooners) somewhere in the Straits of Fuca and Georgia. In the background, Mount Baker.

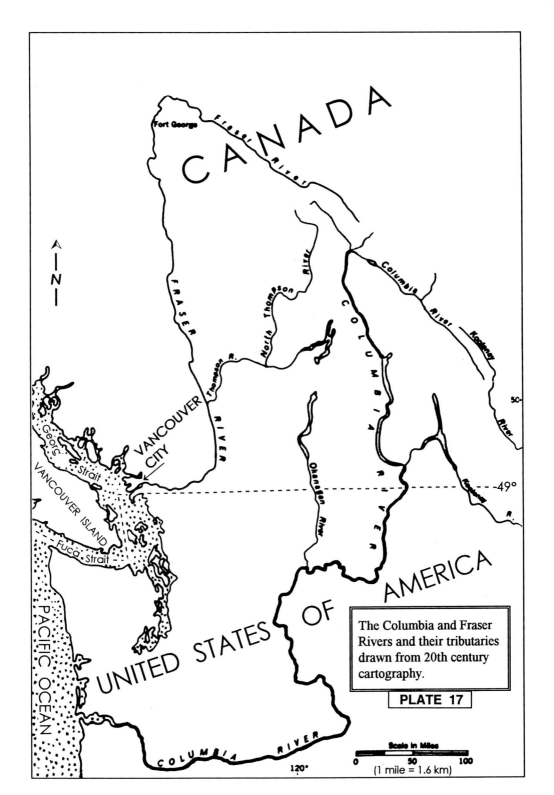

The Columbia and Fraser
Rivers and their tributaries
drawn from 20th century
cartography.

PLATE 17

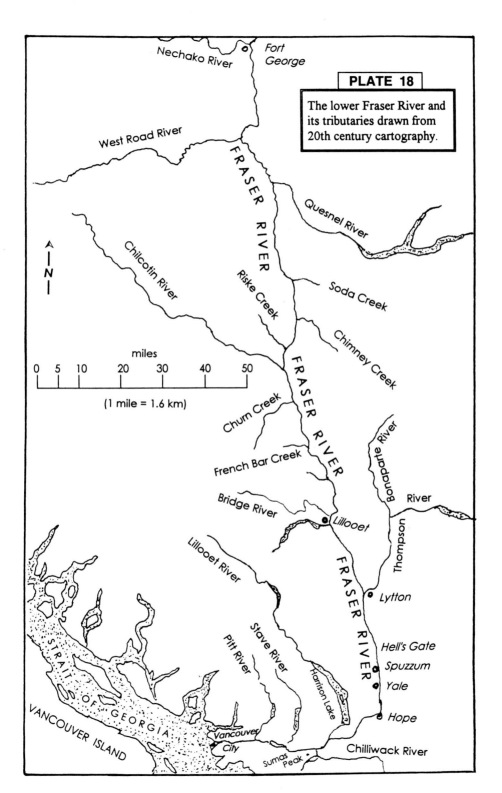

Nechako River

Fort
George

PLATE 18

The lower Fraser River and
its tributaries drawn from
20th century cartography.

West Road River

F R A S E R   R I V E R

Quesnel River

N

Chicotin River

Riske Creek

Soda Creek

miles

0 5 10   20   30   40   50

(1 mile = 1.6 km)

Chimney Creek

F R A S E R   R I V E R

Churn Creek

French Bar Creek

Bonaparte River

Bridge River

River

Lillooet

Thompson

Lillooet River

F R A S E R   R I V E R

Lytton

Pitt River

Stave River

Harrison Lake

Hell's Gate

Spuzzum

Yale

Hope

STRAIT   O F   GEORGIA

VANCOUVER ISLAND

Vancouver
City

Sumas
Peak

Chilliwack River

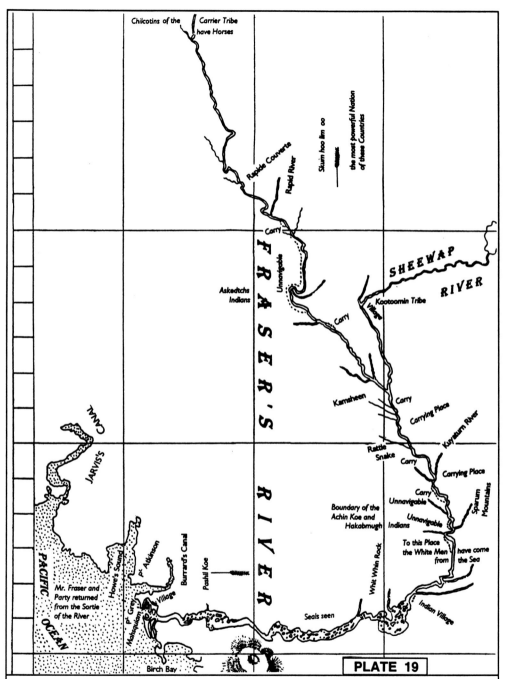

Chikcotins of the
Carrier Tribe
have Horses

Rapide Couverte

Rapid River

Skuin hoo lim oo

the most powerful Nation
of these Countries

Carry

SHEEWAP

RIVER

Unnavigable

Askedtchs
Indians

Kootoomin Tribe

Carry

Village

Kamsheen

Carry

Carrying Place

Kuysaum River

FRASER'S

Rattle
Snake

Carry

Carrying Place

Carry

JARVIS'S CANAL

Unnavigable

Spazum
Mountains

Boundary of the
Achin Koe and
Hakabmugh

Unnavigable

Indians

RIVER

Whit Whin Rock

To this Place
the White Men
from

have come
the Sea

PACIFIC

P^t Atkinson

Burrard's Canal

Pashil Koe

Howe's Sound

Mr. Fraser and
Party returned
from the Sortie
of the River

P^t Grey

Village

Mahquolum

OCEAN

Seals seen

Indian Village

Birch Bay

PLATE 19

Section from David Thompson's *Map of the North-West Territory of the Province of Canada*, drawn in 1813-14, carefully traced from a reduced photocopy of the original, but omitting lines and shadings for mountains and other topographic features. The words are handwritten in the original; here they are printed in their respective locations. Water is indicated by dots.

PLATE 20

Portrait of a Chief of Langara Point, i.e., of Point Grey, drawn by José Cardero of the Alcalá Galiano Expedition in 1792. The earliest portrait of an inhabitant of the zone of what is now Vancouver City.

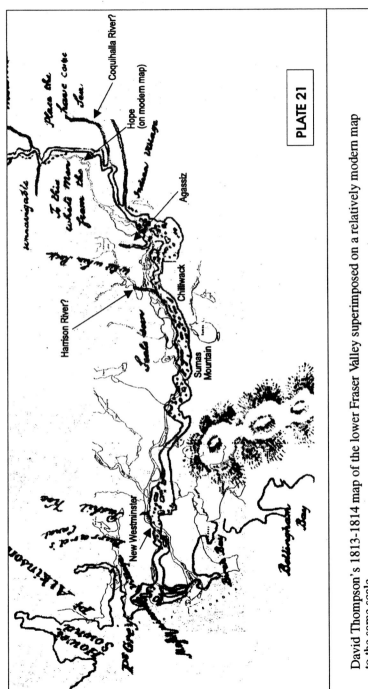

David Thompson's 1813-1814 map of the lower Fraser Valley superimposed on a relatively modern map to the same scale.

The "modern" map shows Sumas Lake, east of Sumas Mountain, which was drained for agriculture in 1922.

PLATE 21

Chapter 8

SEQUEL and OVERVIEW

VANCOUVER'S GROUP RETURNS TO BIRCH BAY

Manby and the launch

On June 20, 1792, the Vancouver-Puget exploring party, with the yawl and the launch, had set out from Jervis Inlet to return to Birch Bay, but the two craft had subsequently become separated. Manby was temporarily in charge of the launch, and his journal reports what happened to him and his companions after they lost sight of the yawl.[77] Two concurrent events concerning fish took place on the following day, at an unspecified location.

First event:

> ...a few hours before my getting to the Ship [that is, before his arrival at Birch Bay] we met a small Indian Fishing Party: they readily bartered five large Sturgeons with us for the buttons off our Jackets.[78]

---

[77] Manby's journal fails to mention where the group spent the night of June 20 to 21, and is in error about the date.

[78] Giving buttons to the Natives was something that Captain James Cook's crew had done during their visit to Nootka Sound in 1778. On that occasion, Cook wrote: "Before we left this place hardly a bit of brass was left in the ship [*Resolution*] except what was in the necessary instruments; whole Suits of clothes were stripped of every button."

The uniforms worn by these members of the British Royal Navy obviously had metal buttons, probably made mostly of brass. Some of the buttons would have been merely decorative, and therefore readily expendable.

Second event: Following the reference to the purchase of fish, Manby's journal states:

> ...at the time of getting this supply we were nearly famished and instantly pulled for the shore in hopes of finding a convenient situation for cooking a meal. In this wish we were disappointed, as it was low water, and a long muddy bank prevented our approaching the shore nearer than a quarter of a mile [460 m].

However, a solution was found to this little difficulty:

> ...at last we had recourse to an immense large tree drifting in the middle of the stream with a great part of its roots many feet above the water. To this friendly tree we gave chase and in an hour made fast our boat alongside and procured a fire capable of roasting an Ox: we boiled a sufficiency, made a luxurious repast and quitted our floating fire after experiencing two hours essential service from it.

Unfortunately Manby's journal does describe in more detail what must have been a delightful scene of a bunch of tired and hungry sailors, tied up to a huge floating tree drifting in the open ocean, building a huge fire on the tree, cooking chunks of fish, and generally having a good time.

This event calls to mind the fact that, two days earlier, the Galiano expedition had been endangered by a huge floating tree, thick, large, and dried-out, and that it had become entangled with the anchor of the *Sutil* as it was moving toward Point Grey. At that time of course, much of the Fraser Valley was still forested, and huge trees must have been frequently swept down to the sea by the river.

After their meal, Manby and his companions continued making for Birch Bay, which they reached about noon that same day, June 21. They found when they got there, that Vancouver and Puget had not yet arrived.

Vancouver's return

Shortly after he and his companions departed from the vicinity of Point Grey at about 9:00 a.m. on June 21 (22 by his reckoning), Vancouver directed his yawl "along the shoals" that he named Sturgeon Bank because it was here that some Native fishermen had sold him "some excellent fish of that kind, weighing from fourteen to two hundred pounds each [to 90 kg]." Puget's journal reports the event with some detail, thus:

> Close to the edge of the Bank our old friends from the Small Village paid us a Visit and brought with them some very fine Sturgeon which we purchased with some pieces of Copper.

By "our old friends from the small village" Puget must have been referring to the village at Noon Breakfast Point (Point Grey) mentioned on page 68. Noticing that the shoals extended all the way to Point Roberts, Vancouver was carefully keeping to their outer edge, a task that was handicapped by the strong tidal and river currents, and a wind that was unfavourable for the desired direction. The party were constantly rowing until 11:00 p.m., when they finally made camp somewhere on the western shore of Point Roberts. The following morning, June 22, they resumed their journey and reached Birch Bay at about noon.

During their return trip to Birch Bay, both Vancouver's group with the yawl, and Manby's group with the launch, had traded metal for fish from the Natives in their canoes, and Manby's group had a eaten well, thanks to the floating tree.

Now that the whole of the Vancouver expedition was together again, the ships were made ready to depart.

The two expeditions meet again

In the morning of the following day, June 23, and in keeping with the agreement they had made, Vancouver and Alcalá Galiano moved toward each other. The ships *Discovery* and *Chatham* left Birch Bay and sailed northward up the Strait of Georgia, while the *Sutil* and *Mexicana* left the vicinity of Point Grey and sailed south. Soon after midday, the four ships were all within sight of each other, and drew closer together. At some stage the Spaniards saluted the British by voicing three cheers, and "the compliment was returned." At about 2:00 p.m., the Spanish ships were brought close enough to the *Chatham* for the two Spanish commanders to go aboard. There they remained "most of the afternoon" while the four vessels sailed northward together.

Alcalá Galiano told Vancouver that some of his men had reconnoitred Burrard Inlet, including Indian Arm, and gave him a copy of the sketch that they had drawn. Although there is no record of their exchanges, the Spanish and British commanders probably briefed each other on their surveys of the area. From this point on, the two expeditions worked for twenty days, more or less cooperatively, exploring the north end of the Strait of Georgia and the inlets around Desolation Sound. Thereafter each expedition went its own way; each navigating by different routes through to Johnstone Strait, Queen Charlotte Strait, around the northern tip of Vancouver Island (Cape Scott), and down the west coast to Nootka.

Discovery and *Chatham* arrived there on August 27–28, 1792. At the time, it was the expectation of the British that all the naval and military personnel of the Spanish establishment would soon return to Mexico, leaving the buildings and other installations intact, and that Broughton, with the *Chatham* and its crew, would remain there, in charge of the establishment on behalf of Great Britain. The Spaniards greeted the Vancouver expedition with great civility, and did what they could in terms of providing equipment and supplies. Puget's journal reports that "a small portion of Vegetables and 2 Sheep with some Milk was sent on board [*Discovery*] and the same compliment was paid to the *Chatham*."

Around midday, August 31, *Sutil* and *Mexicana* arrived, and shortly after began preparations for the voyage back to the Spanish naval base at San Blas. Vancouver's book records that there was a further display of generosity by the Spaniards: "Senrs [Señores] Galiano and Valdes added all they had in their power to spare among which were three excellent goats." This must have meant goats that had been on board *Sutil* or *Mexicana* and, since there were no domestic goats at the places they had visited, goats that had been on board at least since the vessels sailed from Neah Bay on June 8. I imagine that it must have been from these animals that Galiano obtained the milk he gave to *Chatham* when the three vessels met in Boundary Bay on June 13, as mentioned above.

Alcalá Galiano and Vancouver developed much respect for each other, and each expressed it in his written record of events. At the time, their respective nations and governments were at peace. Vancouver died in 1798. Six years later the two nations were at war, and in 1805, near Cape Gibraltar on the southern tip of Spain, their navies fought a battle, during which Cayetano Valdés was wounded and Dionisio Alcalá Galiano was killed.

OVERVIEW

Cartography

Both the Galiano and the Vancouver expeditions produced charts showing the coastlines they had explored. Each added to their work by including contributions from the other. In the case of the Vancouver expedition, charts were drawn by Joseph Baker, under the supervision of Vancouver. One of the charts covers a large segment of the Northwest Coast, including all of Vancouver Island and the adjacent mainland. I call it the <u>Baker chart</u> (Plate 9). This chart was the basis of a second chart which was printed in single sheets and included in the atlas that accompanied Vancouver's book, first published in 1798. I call it the <u>Vancouver chart</u> (Plate 10). Both of these charts include Indian Arm, which was copied from a sketch that Galiano gave to Vancouver. The Vancouver chart covers the Northwest Coast between latitudes 45°30'N and 54°15'N, and has an inset chart of the Columbia River estuary. Although the two charts are the same in many of their details, there are a few differences, but it was the Vancouver chart that became the definitive chart of this part of the world for many years.

The Galiano and Valdés expedition produced sketches and charts showing the coasts that they had surveyed, together with information that they obtained from other charts, such as those of López de Haro, Eliza, and Baker-Vancouver. Subsequently, two editions of this composite were printed; the first in 1795, the second as part of an atlas to accompany the book *Relación*, published in 1802. Each includes the whole of Vancouver Island, the adjacent continental coast, and the lowest segment of the Columbia River. Summarizing: the aforementioned charts are:

> Baker, drawn in 1792–4 (unpublished)
> Galiano, published in 1795
> Vancouver, published in 1798
> Galiano (2nd edition), published in 1802.

The parts of these charts that show the Vancouver area are included here, along with a corresponding extract from a modern chart.

Toponyms

Vancouver's chart shows five relevant toponyms, namely, Point Roberts, Roberts Bank, Sturgeon Bank, Burrard's Canal, and Point Atkinson. Vancouver's book mentions the attribution of all of these toponyms, which have become official designations, the only difference being that Burrard's Canal is now known as Burrard Inlet which includes parts both east and west of the First Narrows.

The toponyms shown on the charts by Galiano and Valdés show some differences between editions, and between them and the accompanying text (See Appendix 3). Retained from the Eliza chart is *Punta de San Rafael* (Punta abbreviated as P^{ta}). What the Eliza chart shows as *Isla de Zepeda* and *Isla(s) de Lángara* become, respectively, *Punta de Cepeda* and *Punta de Lángara*. What the Eliza chart shows as *Boca de Florida Blanca* disappears, and rightly so. In the Galiano chart of 1795, the whole of Burrard Inlet is labelled *Brazo de Florida Blanca* (*brazo* meaning arm). In the Galiano chart of 1802, it is labelled *Canal de Sasamat*. (See Appendix 4.)

Drawings

Drawing was one of the many skills required of sailors in Vancouver's time, views of ports seen from the sea being important navigational aids. The Vancouver expedition, by good luck, had a few participants who were quite skilled at this art. They drew a number of sketches in the general area of the Juan de Fuca Strait and the Strait of Georgia, although none are directly pertinent to the site of the city of Vancouver.

The Galiano expedition included José Cardero, officially serving in the capacity of draughtsman or artist. In the course of the expedition's survey of the two straits and their inlets, he drew several sketches of Indigenous people, sites, and at least one village. Galiano and Valdés testified that he devoted much time and care to this work, and that he participated in all the trips effected by the expedition's launch. If this last statement is strictly true, then Cardero was one of the Spaniards who, with a launch and a boat reconnoitred the whole of Burrard Inlet; however, only one of Cardero's drawings (shown in Plate 20) is specifically related to this locale.

The drawing is a portrait of a man donned with a hat of the kind that were worn by chiefs of some other parts of the Northwest coast. The drawing has a title to the effect that the man was Chief of *Punta de Lángara,* that is Point Grey; the implication being that a chief of the Native community dwelling near Point Grey posed for Cardero. There is however, some uncertainty about this portrait. The expedition's records refer to only one chief near Point Grey, specifying that he was old and was wearing a hat. While the subject of Cardero's portrait is wearing a hat, he does not look old. Either Cardero failed to convey the chief's age, or else he was another chief not mentioned in the expedition's records. Whatever the truth of the matter, this is the only existing portrait of a resident of the Vancouver area prior to the mid-nineteenth century.

Some of Cardero's drawings and those of the British can help form a general idea of the appearance of the habitations and the inhabitants of the shores of the Juan de Fuca Strait and the Strait of Georgia before the arrival of Europeans.

Facts and circumstances

About the Spanish explorations by the Eliza and the Galiano expeditions, little was published in Spain or elsewhere. This remained the case for many years. In contrast, information about Vancouver's explorations was widely published and several editions and translations of his book were produced. None of these charts however showed anything of the Fraser River.

After 1792, citizens of several countries, mainly Britain and the United States, continued calling at different parts of the Northwest Coast to trade for sea-otter furs. The fur-trading companies based in central Canada continued extending their field of operations westward toward the Pacific coast, with the full support of the British government. At the same time, the government of the United States began showing a serious interest in the west and gave support to American citizens engaged in trade on the Pacific coast and in the Columbia River delta. Great Britain and the United States were becoming rivals in the region, while the power of Spain to exercise any effective authority gradually diminished.

THE RIVERS FRASER AND COLUMBIA

Missing the Fraser River?

Presumably, Narváez, Vancouver, and Galiano would have liked to have surveyed the approximately thirty-five kilometres of coast between Point Roberts and Point Grey more thoroughly than they did. They were very much aware of the shoals and mudbanks flanking the shoreline, and apparently they did not get close to the several mouths of the Fraser River.

There is little existing information on how much time and effort Narváez put into surveying the estuary in 1791, although his sketch has some interesting detail, but we have a much better idea of how long Vancouver and Galiano were within sight of that part of the coast.

On June 11: Vancouver and Puget navigated their way along the stretch, starting from the tip of Point Roberts, until they were obliged to turn westward and thus lose sight of the shore. The moon that day was in its last quarter and so the (neap) tide was not especially high or low throughout the day.

On June 13: Alcalá Galiano and Valdés, setting out from Boundary Bay, were able to observe some of the coast from Point Roberts to the northward, but they too had to turn west so neither Vancouver and Puget, nor Galiano and Valdés, were able to survey the northern part of Sturgeon Bank. The tide for the most part was moderately high (3 m) and not changing very much.

On June 21: Vancouver and Puget, in full daylight, went from Point Grey to Point Roberts. So they had a chance of looking again at that shoreline, but only from a considerable distance. There had been a new moon on June 19, so the tide at noon was quite low (0.6 m) rising to a high (4.6 m) at about 8:00 p.m.

On June 23: Both expeditions may have had a final opportunity of seeing the coast. The British expedition, while navigating from Birch Bay, on a northward course; the Spanish expedition while navigating from Point Grey on a southward course. Shortly thereafter, as the two expeditions met and proceeded together northward, they had one last chance of observing the coast. At about the time of their departure, the tide was low (1 m).

Altogether, the British spent more time than the Spaniards sailing or rowing up and down the estuary region, and therefore had a better chance of observing the nature of the coast between the two promontories. This is what Vancouver wrote about it:

The intermediate space is occupied by very low land, apparently a swampy flat, that retires several miles, before the country raises to meet the rugged snowy mountains, which we found still continuing in a direction nearly along the coast. This low flat being very much indented, and extending behind Point Roberts, to join the low land in the bay to the eastward of that point [Boundary Bay]; gives its high land, when seen at a distance, the appearance of an island: this, however, is not the case, notwithstanding there are two openings between this point and Point Grey. These can only be navigable by canoes, as the shoal continues along the coast to the distance of seven or eight miles [14 km] from the shore, on which were lodged, and especially before these openings, logs of wood and stumps innumerable.

And this is what Puget wrote:

...the land to the Eastward is low and about three leagues Distant [17 km]. Two places in that Direction bear much the Appearance of Large Rivers but the Shoals hitherto have prevented any Communication with them.

About the same coastal stretch the Spaniards wrote that *Punta de Lángara*, that is Point Grey, was high ground and so was the coast that followed from there on the southeastern trend for about half a mile (925 m) and "its continuation" was very low and swampy with no hills until the end of the *Cepeda Peninsula* (Point Roberts).[79]

It is clear that Vancouver and Puget, and to a lesser extent Galiano and Valdés as well, noticed indications of the mouths of a river between Point Grey and Point Roberts. The Eliza chart also very clearly shows entrances. However, I have carefully researched the records of both of the 1792 expeditions and have not found in any of them a specific and clear statement to the effect that there was a major river estuary in that part of North America, nor is there any specification of it in the charts produced by these explorers.

---

[79] John Work, who was a member of the first expedition of Europeans to navigate the south arm of the Fraser wrote: "The land about the entrance of the river is very low and swampy with some few scattered pines of a small size and bushes....The sea on each side of the entrance of this River appears to be shallow."

A book on the Northwest Coast published in Canada in 1924, after mentioning that Vancouver, when departing from Point Grey to return to Boundary Bay, acquired some sturgeon from local Natives, comments:

> Now Vancouver and his sailors must have known that the sturgeon frequents the mouths and lower reaches of rivers. What perverse impulse of darkness beclouded their vision and reasoning powers on this their second opportunity to locate the river mouths!

Dr. John Norris, professor emeritus of history, who has had long experience in navigation and knows very well the geography of this area, comments:

> The explorers, Spanish and British, were experienced navigators. They could identify outfalls of rivers quite easily from the evidence of the low salinity of the water (scientifically measurable by the 1790s), the flood of silt in the summer, the current, and the topography of the coast line—all of which are and were easily observable in the case of the Fraser. The ships themselves were not used for inshore surveys in any case. These were the duty of officers in small sailing or rowing boats. The argument that shoals prevented the vessels coming sufficiently inshore to observe the Fraser is doubly nonsensical: the presence of the sandbars was evidence of a river; the small boats were of sufficiently shallow draft to enable them to come inshore, sandbars or no sandbars. The flood of the Fraser in summer is easily observable, well out into the Strait of Georgia. The truth is that Vancouver missed all three of the great rivers of the area: the Columbia, the Fraser, and the Skeena which has an enormous estuary. We need to examine what these explorers were looking for to understand why they missed the Fraser.

When, in the afternoon of June 23, Alcalá Galiano went aboard the ship *Discovery*, it had already been agreed that the two expeditions would cooperate in further exploration. Since the Spaniards had told Vancouver that they suspected the existence of a major river in the area, and since Vancouver and Puget had noticed indications of river mouths, the two expeditions could have taken the opportunity of using their boats to approach the shore and establish the presence of the river mouths. Such a "discovery" might have prompted a much earlier exploration and charting of at least the last few miles of the river's course. None of this occurred, and the earliest exploration of the Fraser was destined to be done, not from the ocean by people in ships, but from the river's upper levels by people who had travelled across the continent from the east in canoes.

*****

The two rivers

As can be seen in Plate 17, the Fraser and the Columbia Rivers spring from the Rocky Mountains and run, on almost parallel lines, in a southward course before turning westward, toward the ocean. The history of the exploration of the Fraser River is closely linked to that of the Columbia.

Around the turn of the eighteenth century, the North West Company was in the fur-trading business, shipping furs across the Atlantic Ocean to Great Britain. There, as well as in other parts of Europe, there was much demand for Canadian fur. The Company knew that ships that acquired pelts from Natives on the northwestern coast of America, crossed the Pacific Ocean to the ports of Macao and Canton in China where there was also a lively market for furs. This trade, the Company realized, offered them a good business opportunity. If they could find a way to bring furs down to the Pacific coast from their territories in the western part of what is now Canada, they too could ship furs to China and Europe, and at the same time could receive supplies for their operations by a cheaper route than the overland route from central Canada. Company employees were therefore actively seeking a way by river to the western sea.

In their westward advance from the central parts of what is now Canada, the fur traders reached some upper valleys of the Rocky Mountains in the region of the Peace River. Here they set up fortified outposts, forts, for storing supplies and trading with the Native people of the region. Such was Fort Fork (or Forks), close to the junction of the Peace and the Smoky Rivers.

In May 1792, the aforementioned Robert Gray, citizen of the United States, commanding the ship *Columbia Rediviva* entered the river, which now bears part of his ship's name, the Columbia River. Subsequently, at Nootka, he reported this event to the Vancouver expedition and to Spanish navigators. In October of that year, William Broughton, of the Vancouver expedition, commanding the vessel *Chatham*, entered the mouth of the Columbia River and proceeded upstream for about eighty-four miles (155 km); that is, up to about the location of what is now the town of Vancouver, in Washington State. (Vancouver's book, first published some six years later, reports this event.)

In 1793, and under the auspices of the North West Company, a party led by its employee Alexander Mackenzie set out from Fort Fork, aiming to find a route to the Pacific coast: trekking, canoeing, portaging, as need be, they went up the Peace River and then crossed the continental divide in the Rocky Mountains. There they came upon another river and followed its course downstream, approximately as far as the site of the present day town of Alexandria. This river was the Fraser. Mackenzie occasionally called it *Great River*, but understood the Natives to call it *Tacoutche Tesse* and to state that, farther downstream, it was impassable for canoes. Consequently, he and his companions changed their plans and, following the Bella Coola River, they reached the waters of the Pacific Ocean at Dean Channel (lat. 52°33'N long. 127°13'W) on July 22, 1793. From local Natives, Mackenzie learned that, some days earlier, another stranger, whose name they pronounced approximately as "Ban-co-bah," had already been there, by ship from the ocean. This stranger was of course George Vancouver, whose book records his visit to the place.

The arduous adventure of Mackenzie and his companions constitutes the earliest recorded case of men travelling between the American heartland and the Pacific coast north of the 40th degree of latitude. However, Mackenzie's route was too difficult to be used for the trade that the North West Company had in mind.

In 1795, as a result of rather vague agreements between Great Britain and Spain, the latter dismantled its establishment at Nootka. The following year marks the end of activity on the Northwest coast on the part of Spain.

During the last years of the eighteenth century, Alexander Mackenzie became acquainted with Vancouver's book and charts, learned that Gray had probed the mouth of the Columbia, and that Broughton had ascended it for some distance. Mackenzie concluded that the Columbia was probably the one he had occasionally called Great River, or Tacoutche Tesse. In 1801, he published a book, illustrated with maps, describing his explorations and related matters. The maps include a river designated as "Tacoutche or Columbia River," delineated as if the upper parts of the two rivers now called Columbia and Fraser joined and formed a single river running down to the Pacific. In his book (page 415), Mackenzie advocates expanding the British fur trade in North America by using rivers for transportation. "The Tacoutche or Columbia River," he states, "flows from the Rocky Mountains and discharges itself in the Pacific at latitude 46°20'N. It is the only navigable river in the whole extent of Vancouver's minute survey of the coast," and this river could provide an excellent link for "intercourse between the Pacific and the Atlantic Oceans."

Such were Mackenzie's notions, based largely on Vancouver's book and charts. His misconception about the Fraser and the Columbia was also reflected in a map printed in England in 1800, which has a dotted line connecting what it labels "Tacoutche or Columbia R[ivers]" with the mouth of what it labels "Oregon or Columbia R[iver]."

During the years 1803–6, an expedition sponsored by the President of the United States, Thomas Jefferson, and led by Meriwether Lewis and William Clark, explored territory west of the Mississippi River, crossed the Rockies, and ascertained the course of the <u>lower</u> part of the Columbia River from latitude 49°N to its mouth. They did not however explore its upper section. News of this exploration spread widely, long before it was reported in detail in a book published in 1815. The Lewis and Clark expedition was an added spur to moves on the part of the United States to establish its sovereignty over the western side of the North American continent.

*****

Thus far, the idea persisted that the Columbia and the Tacoutche Tesse River were one. It became a matter of great interest to fur traders and governments alike to know the true relationship between these rivers. In 1808, Simon Fraser found the answer, but it was not what anyone had expected.

Chapter 9

SIMON FRASER EXPLORES THE FRASER RIVER
(1808)

In November 1804, the Hudson's Bay Company and the North West Company agreed to amalgamate; however, they continued to operate separately until 1821. Simon Fraser, of the North West Company, accepted as correct Mackenzie's notion that the river, then called Tacoutche Tesse, was actually the upper waters of the Columbia River. Between 1805 and 1807, starting from Rocky Mountain House on the North Saskatchewan River, he explored the neighbouring land, and set up trading outposts for the company. One such post, called Fort George, was on the site of what is now the town of Prince George, at the confluence of the Nechako and Fraser Rivers.

Fraser made plans to explore the river from Fort George all the way to its mouth, assuming this to be on the Pacific coast, at latitude 46°20'N. In the autumn of 1807, he received orders from the North West Company to proceed with the exploration, which he did, accompanied and assisted by other men, the following year.

He knew from experience that along the river he was likely to encounter Native people, some of whom might be of assistance to him. Fraser spoke English and also French, and probably had some words of various Native languages.

The composition of Fraser's party was the usual one for the fur traders of the time. There were two clerks, Jules Quesnel and John Stuart, both fellow employees of the North West Company, and nineteen paddlers, or *voyageurs*, eight French-Canadians who are named in Fraser's Report, and two Native North Americans. The two Natives knew some of the local languages and were expected to provide guidance and linguistic help in contacts with local people along the river banks. Thus, twenty-four men formed the expeditionary group.

They were in for very hard times, that required enormous strength and endurance. Fraser was thirty-two years old, Stewart was twenty-nine, and Quesnel only twenty-two. Presumably the rest of the men were fairly young too. In any case, the whole group proved to be up to the task.

Records

The group recorded events and described the river's features. Stuart was in charge of assessing and of recording in a logbook, data about the course of the river, distances, longitude and latitude reckonings, etc. This required special instruments and much technical skill. Perhaps Stuart had them. In any case he kept such a log, but it no longer exists. During the adventure Fraser wrote notes. From them, from data in Stuart's log, and probably by adding something from memory, he eventually wrote an account that constitutes the only existing firsthand document about the journey.[80] It seems that there are no other documents that can provide substantial additional information, and that the party did not draw any chart of the course of the river, nor sketches that would provide visual aids about the territories they crossed and the peoples they met. Like many documents of a similar kind, Fraser's narrative raises problems as to the identity of villages, tribes, topographic features, etc.

As explained in Chapter 10, David Thompson, who was employed by the North West Company, had access to Stuart's log, and probably to Fraser's narrative as well. On the basis of this information, plus explorations he himself carried out over many years, Thompson drew a map which encompasses a very vast territory that includes the course of both the Fraser and Columbia Rivers. The map is inscribed with place-names and notes that provide much help in understanding the events of Fraser's exploration.

Such is the nature of the data that may be considered firsthand. On the basis of them, books and papers have been written by L.R. Masson, H.H. Bancroft, E.O.S. Scholefield, F.W. Howay, Walter N. Sage, Bruce Hutchinson, and a few others. The full text of Fraser's reports, plus background information, biographic data, notes and commentaries, was published by W. Kaye Lamb in

---

[80] Actually, two accounts still exist. One covers the whole of the expedition, and one covers only ten days of it. Both are printed in Lamb's book. The original of the long account is in the Toronto Public Library.

1960. (See Bibliography.) At least two of these various publications contain assertions for which there is no documentary basis. As mentioned above, I do not include in this work details that can not be found in the firsthand data, but on matters or details on which there is no such information I dare make suppositions, but only while making it clear to the reader that I am so doing. This is very much the case in this chapter, mainly because Fraser's narrative has many points that I find unclear or confusing.

Preparations

There is no existing thoroughly-documented information about preparations for the voyage and about the equipment used. Some details are mentioned, here and there, in Fraser's narrative, and some others may be inferred from what information that still exists about Mackenzie's explorations and about activities of European personnel in the region then called New Caledonia.[81] With a documentary basis for most of the items, and what I consider justifiable deductions about others, I offer the following exposition about the initial expedition's equipment and related matters.

Four birch bark canoes, very suitable for navigation in narrow or turbulent rivers; some birch bark pieces and other materials for repairing the canoes; kettles and other cooking utensils; tobacco; first-aid kit; some medicines, including Turlington balsam and laudanum;[82] small camping tents in pieces that could be folded; large sheets of oilcloth (canvas) that could cover the equipment in the canoes, to protect it from rain, and could also be used for accommodating the group ashore, especially for sleeping purposes; nets and other fishing gear; compasses and a sextant; a small portable writing desk containing paper, quill, and ink; firearms, bullets, and gun powder; containers

---

[81] It would appear that Fraser's party expected that in the course of the exploration they would cache edibles such as smoked salmon, and obtain fish and some edible vegetables from their own effort and also from Natives they would encounter. In payment for such items, or in return for favours, or as presents to earn good will, the party would give some articles to the Natives; so the equipment should include some such articles.

The book by Marjorie Wilkins Campbell has some details on the equipment, and though it does not specify documentary basis on which it is based, I think the details are basically correct.

[82] In the course of his exploratory trips Mackenzie had administered "a few drops of Turlington's balsam in some water."

made of buffalo horns, for keeping gunpowder; perhaps needles and thread for repairing shoes and mending garments; articles meant primarily to be given, for whatever reason, to people encountered during the trip: knives, beads, cottonwoods, calico blankets; for nutrition: dried salmon, perhaps pemmican,[83] probably some tea and chocolate (the latter perhaps only for Fraser and the two clerks); "high wines"; and at least "one small keg of shrub," a beverage that consisted of fruit juice, sugar, and rum or other alcoholic base. Each man had an outfit that, packed in a tight roll, could be carried under the canoe seats. Contents? A couple of blankets; a change of buckskin shirt and breeches; extra moccasins; and a coloured sash or *ceinture flechée* for dress-up occasions. Most of the men had a knife, a dagger, and a rifle with ammunition. Fraser and some others, perhaps all, had a "calumet" pipe, long stemmed, probably ornamented, and a bag for keeping pipe and tobacco.

The existing data does not specify whether or not Fraser had charts from the recent coastal explorations, but his report reveals that he knew the approximate latitude of the mouth of the Columbia, and was aware of the existence of the Strait of Georgia, but perhaps not of its exact shape and size.

In connection with what his report says, or does not say, concerning the lower parts of the Fraser River and its surroundings, it should be borne in mind:
- the river has its annual freshet between May and August;
- Fraser reconnoitred its lower parts in the course of June and July; that is, when the river is high;
- it is likely that the river was in flood and that, consequently, parts of the terrain looked like islands.

THE EXPLORATION

In the following account of Fraser's exploration, I make only a few references to the upper parts of the river, but mention most of what Fraser

---

[83] Here is a definition of pemmican from Webster's dictionary, 1957 edition:
"Among the North American Indians, lean buffalo meat or venison cut in thin slices, dried in the sun, pounded fine, mixed with melted fat, and packed in sacks of buffalo hide. Also a similar preparation to which fruit is sometimes added, used by explorers, etc. It is often compressed and contains much nutriment in small compass."

recorded about events, tribes, villages, houses, etc., in territories between the junction with its tributary, the Thompson River, and its termination in the Strait of Georgia. That is, details that may help form an idea of facts and circumstances in the area of present-day Greater Vancouver and its vicinity, many years before Europeans began to settle in it.

The exploration started on May 28, 1808,[84] from Fort George, by the party paddling their canoes downstream. Occasionally, they camped ashore and pitched tent for the night. In some places they caught salmon and other fish. On occasion, discovering unguarded food in some inhabited place, they took some but left something else, as token payment. They encountered many Natives, especially in groups, and the contacts were facilitated by the two Indians in the party who knew some of the local languages. It seems that most of the groups encountered realized that the strangers, despite carrying weapons, did not mean to harm them. Some communities, and a number of individuals, acted in a hostile way toward these strangers, and a few actually harassed them. However, it was largely because of help provided by the Natives that the main objectives of the expedition were achieved.

Most communities had canoes very suited to navigating the river. In its upper parts, light canoes, mostly made of birch bark; in rather flat regions, heavier canoes made from huge and broad cedar logs. Some canoes were very long and, altogether, capable of carrying the twenty-four expedition members, plus other persons. Some tribes of the Cariboo-Chilcotin region had horses. Nearly all tribes had the kind of "wool" dog[85] whose very long hair was used for weaving blankets and rugs. Some tribes seemed to be fairly prosperous, others less so. Most appeared to have leaders or chiefs who exerted authority. There were cases of persons kept as slaves. There were various languages, some very different from others. Some tribes had notions about men from other parts having come to neighbouring regions. Some knew that the river reached the sea. On its upper parts, some tribes owned articles that had obviously come from the east, through the activities of the North West Company. In the Fraser canyon they saw evidence of smallpox. On lower parts, some communities had articles that in all probability had come, originally, from fur-trading ships that visited the Northwest Coast. Surely, such exotic articles must have been

---

[84] Fraser's original manuscript has an error on this date, as explained in Lamb's edition.

[85] Now extinct, probably the kind mentioned on pages 104, 128, and 130.

acquired by Native people of distant parts and changed hands through the process of intertribal trade, thus reaching upper regions of the river before any "white" people appeared there.

From the beginning, Fraser cached some salmon and other things at convenient locations, expecting to return and retrieve them; in one place he left two canoes ashore, and some supplies under a pile of brush. On occasion, he was able to borrow or to buy one or two canoes from Natives, or else have his group transported by Natives in such craft, for some distance. In at least one place, helpful Natives sent word to other Natives dwelling further down the river, to expect and assist the strangers' party, as was actually done.

Fraser recorded names of some Native Nations and tribes, and specified the location of some of their villages and camps. A number of them have been identified; Thompson's map is very helpful in this respect.

Some Natives provided information, more or less accurate, about the river. At one time, meeting Native people who had heard about the existence of firearms and were curious about their use, the voyagers "fired several shots, the report of which astonished them to that degree as to make them drop off their legs." Using a gun from the explorers, one Native person fired it, just to try it, and the bullet nearly hit some of his companions standing nearby. The explorers never fired at anybody, but when badly harassed they would make a demonstration of force with their guns.

Because the river has narrows and rapids in some stretches, the explorers were unable to canoe it all the way. At such locations they had to walk painfully along the river banks, occasionally incurring considerable risks. At some stage Natives advised the party to get off the banks altogether, trek on land for a considerable distance, and then return to the river. This was never done because Fraser was anxious to reconnoitre the whole of its course.

Fraser's group successfully reached the river delta and estuary, close to the present-day city of Vancouver; however, the inhabitants treated them so roughly that they spent very little time there. Thus, what Fraser recorded about his visit to this spot mostly concerns confrontations, and it says very little about the one village that he visited there, Musqueam, and nothing about the Native way of life.

From the site of Lytton to the river delta

Now for details about the late stages of the exploration. All the quotations in the rest of this chapter are from Fraser's narrative, as printed in the aforementioned book edited by W. Kaye Lamb. For the sake of convenience, two villages are designated as *Chief's Village* and *Village X*.

June 19:   Fraser and his companions reached, at the site of present-day Lytton, the junction of the Fraser River and a river that Fraser named the Thompson River in honour of his friend David Thompson.[86] The following day the explorers were joined by an Indian of the Hacamaugh [*Nlaka'pamux*] Nation (the people of the Fraser Canyon and the Thompson River). Fraser's narrative first mentions him as "a little fellow from whom we received much attention"; subsequently, it mentions him simply as "little fellow," and states that he was very helpful, but it does not give his actual name. In the following pages he is referred to as *Little Fellow*.

June 21–26:   Fraser and his companions now had to make their way through the famous Fraser Canyon. There were parts where local inhabitants had traditional ways and means of climbing the canyon walls by trails that made use of every flat ledge there was. In parts not otherwise accessible, they had used tree trunks and willow branches to construct ladders that hung from rocks and stumps. With considerable help from local inhabitants, Fraser and his companions were able to get past the canyon. At one spot a Native climbed up to the top of a cliff, and by means of a long pole, pulled them up, one by one. The canoes were "turned adrift and left to the mercy of the current" and later recovered, very damaged, below the rapids.

June 27:   The group reached a camp at a place called *Spazum* (Spuzzum), which is the beginning of the end of the canyon about 17 km above Yale. From Yale, the Fraser is easily navigable to the sea.

June 28:   "After much trouble both by land and water," the voyagers left their canoes and baggage ashore, proceeded on foot, and reached a village where they were very well treated by the inhabitants. Fraser considered them to be "of

---

[86] The compliment was returned for it was Thompson who formalized the name Fraser River.

the Ackinroe nation"[87] that was "different in language and in manners from the other nations" he had come upon. The village had about 140 inhabitants, who treated the explorers lavishly. Fraser assumed "from their workmanship in wood" that these people had "good tools, at least for this purpose" [for wood cutting, carving, etc.]. They also had "very neat" bows and arrows; nets, eight fathoms long (14.6 m), for catching deer and other large animals; rugs made from the wool of wild goat, and from dog hair; and also rugs "which are equally as good as those found in Canada," that is, the then growing Canada, far away to the east of the Rocky Mountains. A phrase in his narrative indicates that Fraser, who was of course an employee of a trading company, endeavoured to find out whether, through intertribal trade, things produced in Canada or in industrial centres elsewhere, reached these inhabitants of the far west of the continent. The phrase is that he saw "few or no Christian goods among them," obviously equating Christianity with Europeans, and not precisely specifying whether or not he actually saw any such goods in this village.

At some distance from the village there was "an excellent house 46 by 23 feet [14 by 7 m], and constructed like American frame houses." The planks were 3 or 4 inches [9 cm] thick, each passing the adjoining one a couple of inches [5 cm]. Very strong and rudely carved posts received the beam across. The walls were 11 feet [3.4 m] high, and supported a slanting roof. It would seem that this was a single building, located between two villages, as Fraser's report adds that at some distance from this house there was "a considerable village" with similar houses, but there is no indication that the voyagers visited it.

In the afternoon, they arrived at a site that has been reckoned to be that of the present-day Yale, where there was "a camp containing about 150 souls" at a spot where the river was "more than two miles [3.2 km] broad, and interspersed with islands" (presumably including temporary islands resulting from the freshet). In the camp, the explorers ate "plenty of Salmon cooked by means of hot stones in wooden vessels"; that is, by a cooking procedure apparently commonly used in the Pacific Northwest mentioned in Chapter 2.

---

[87] Fraser was passing into the territory of the Stó:lō Nation. The Stó:lō (river) people belong to one of the linguistic groupings called Coast Salish (*Halq'emeylem*). The people in and above the canyon speak languages in the Interior Salish family. The word "Achinroe" is a rendering of the Interior Salish word for the *Halq'emeylem*.

Regarding the inhabitants and their way of life, Fraser's narrative contains the following detail: "They have scarcely any leather, so that large animals must be scarce." As ornaments, they had shells of different kinds; shell beads, brass made into pipes hanging from the neck, or across the shoulders; bracelets of brass wire, and some made of horn; hats made of wattap roots, which had broad rims, diminishing gradually at the top, etc. There was "a new tomb supported on carved posts about two feet [60 cm] from the ground," and the posts were covered all over with bright shells which shone like mercury. Then the narrative has these remarks:

> Both sexes are stoutly made, and some of the men are handsome; but
> I cannot say much of the women, who seem to be slaves, for in the
> course of their dances, I remarked that the men were pillaging them
> from one another. Our Little Fellow, on one of these occasions, was
> presented with another man's wife for a bed fellow.[88]

Fraser understood these people to say that "white people" had come to this region "from below," which seems to mean, enigmatically, that Europeans coming from the lower Fraser, or from the Pacific Ocean, had reached so far inland. In a reference to the inhabitants of that village, he recorded:

> ...they shewed us indented marks that the white people made upon the
> rocks, but which...seemed to us to be natural marks.

Perhaps the marks were natural as Fraser thought, or they may have been made by the Natives themselves, for there is ample evidence of their ability to carve petroglyphs. On the other hand, it is all but sure that no white people had ever visited the camp or been in the vicinity of what is now Yale. It seems that it was there that the explorers spent the night of June 28.

June 29: The explorers continued canoeing downstream and stopped at "a camp on an island" with about 125 inhabitants and, later, at "another camp of 170 souls," where they spent the night. The first camp is thought to have been

---

[88] This suggests that Little Fellow fornicated with a married woman provided by her husband. However, since there is evidence of slavery amongst these tribes, perhaps the woman was a slave, and not that man's wife, but his lover or mistress.

near Hope; the second at Ruby Creek.[89]   Regarding the local inhabitants, Fraser noted:

> The Indians in this quarter are fairer than those in the interior. Their heads and faces are extremely flat; their skin and hair of a reddish cast—but this cast, I suppose, is owing to the ingredients with which they besmear their bodies. They make rugs, of Dog's hair, that have stripes of different colours crossing at right angles resembling, at a distance, Highland [Scottish] plaid. Their fishing nets are of large twine, and have handles of 20 feet [6 m] [length].

These people had two objects that must have intrigued the visitors: a large copper kettle shaped like a jar, and a large english hatchet stamped *Sargaret*, with the figure of a crown.

<u>June 30:</u> Navigating in borrowed canoes, accompanied by their owners, the explorers arrived at "a camp containing near 400 souls."   Subsequently, continuing their course downstream, they reached a spot

> where the river expands into a lake. Here we saw seals, a large river coming in from the left, and a round Mountain ahead, which the Natives call *Shemotch* [?]. After sunset we encamped upon the right side of the river. At this place the trees are remarkably large, cedars five fathoms (9.1 m) in circumference, and of proportional height. Mosquitoes are in clouds, and we had little or nothing to eat. The Natives always gave us plenty of provisions in their villages, but nothing to carry away. Numbers of them followed us, but were as destitute of provisions as ourselves. And though they were a great distance from home, they carried no arms about them.

It is likely that there was no actual and permanent lake there, but that because of the freshet the river looked much wider than usual. The location was probably upstream of Chilliwack near Agassiz where the Fraser valley finally opens out. The "round Mountain" was perhaps Sumas Mountain; it could not have been Mount Baker because this is not visible east of Abbotsford and also because it is peaked, not "round[ed]."

---

[89]   Howay was definite about the location of the second camp, as he wrote, "Fraser reembarked on June 29th and that night encamped near a large village which was situated at what we now call Ruby Creek."

The "large river coming in from the left," was perhaps the Chilliwack River which joins the Fraser across from Nicomen Island, although it is not really large, or perhaps the explorers were referring to the stream flowing from the nearby shallow, but extensive Sumas Lake (now drained). It is odd in the light of this remark that the existence of the Stave River, Pitt River, and Harrison River, all of which flow into the Fraser from the right (north), is not in the least bit reflected in Simon Fraser's report. Thompson's map however, does show rivers not mentioned in the report, some in surprising detail, the Coquihalla River for example.[90]

Thompson's map is inscribed "Seals seen" at a spot that presumably corresponds to where Fraser saw harbour seals in the river.

<u>July 1:</u> The travellers visited a village. Fraser's report does not provide its name and does not specify its location: this is the one I call *Chief's Village*. Following is the entry in the report for that day:

> Foggy weather this morning. Clear at 4:00 a.m. and we embarked. Rugged Mountains all around. The banks of the river are low and well covered with wood; the current is slack.
>
> At 8:00 a.m. we arrived at a large village. After shaking hands with many, the chief invited us to his house, and served us with fish and berries; our Indians [the two Native people in Fraser's group] were also treated with fish, berries and dried oysters in large troughs...
>
> The Indians entertained us with songs and dances of various descriptions. The chief stood in the centre of the dance or ring giving directions, while others were beating the drum against the walls of the house, and making a terrible racket—which alarmed our men who were at a distance, and who came to see what caused the noise...
>
> The number of Indians in this place is about two hundred, who appeared at first to be fair, but afterwards we discovered that they made use of white paint to alter their appearance. They evinced no

---

[90]   Perhaps it should be added that Thompson's map of the lower reaches of the Fraser (Plate 21) shows two rivers flowing in from the left; one that seems to be at Hope where the Fraser turns westward (the Coquihalla); and another shortly after (Fraser's "large river"?) where the valley is narrow and there are only creeks. On the right (north) side, there is an unidentifiable "blip," just below the inscription *Pashil Koe*. Further east, to the east of the "seals seen" annotation is what <u>could</u> be the Harrison. To the east of that, in the vicinity of the "lake," is drawn a river near Agassiz where there are today only sloughs (Maria, Mountain, etc.).

kind of surprise or curiosity at seeing us, nor were they afraid of our arms, so that they must have been in the habit of seeing white people.[91]

Their houses are built of cedar planks, and in shape similar to the one already described. [the one seen three days earlier, mentioned above] The whole range, which is 640 feet [195 m] long by 60 [18 m] broad, is under one roof. The front is 18 feet [5.5 m] high, and the covering is slanting. All the apartments, which are separated in portions, are square, excepting the chief's which is 90 feet [27 m] long. In this room the posts or pillars are nearly 3 feet [90 cm] diameter at the base, and diminishing gradually to the top. In one of these posts is an oval opening answering the purpose of a door, thro' which to crawl in and out. Above, on the outside, are carved a human figure large as life, and there are other figures in imitation of beasts and birds. These buildings have no flooring. The fires are in the centre, and the smoke goes out an opening at [the] top.

The tombs at this place are well finished. Dog's hair, which is spun with a distaff and spindle is formed into rugs. There is some red and blue cloth among them. These Indians are not so hospitable as those above; this is probably owing to scarcity of Provisions.

Unfortunately the sentence about tombs is too vague. The houses were of the kind that was characteristic in that part of North America at that time in history (see Chapter 2).

In the course of the day, the Natives who had transported the explorers in canoes thus far, departed with the canoes. After much difficulty, Fraser obtained the promise that the following morning the local chief would lend the explorers "his large canoe" and would go along with them. So the voyagers spent in the village the night of July 1, in the course of which some dogs "dragged out and damaged" many of their belongings.

July 2: - *Village X*

Early in the morning, the explorers discovered that a smoking bag belonging to them had been stolen, and, despite requests to the local people, they failed to recover it. Furthermore, they had difficulties with the chief they had met the previous day concerning transportation in his large canoe, but eventually the

---

[91] There are good reasons to think that no Europeans had been there before Fraser's visit.

party, accompanied by the chief and other members of his tribe, were able to depart from *Chief's Village* and travel downriver.

At 11:00 a.m. the travellers arrived at another village which, for the sake of identification, I call *Village X*. Its houses were "plain and in two rows." There, Simon Fraser was given "two coats of mail in a present which are so good [for] shoes." This statement suggests the coats were made of leather and that cuts from them could be used for making and repairing footwear.

From another statement in Fraser's narrative, quoted below, it may be inferred that the village was situated about two miles (3.2 km) to the east of the spot on the eastern tip of Lulu Island, where the river divides into several channels. Unfortunately, the narrative does not provide any indication as to what side (north or south?) of the river the village was situated. There were Kwantlen villages both sides of the river, and the sites of some are no longer known with certainty. Perhaps *Village X* was at New Westminster (*Sxwoyimelth*), perhaps it was near Sapperton at the mouth of the Brunette River which is about two miles from Lulu Island, or perhaps it was a few miles farther upstream at the mouth of the Coquitlam River.[92]

The inhabitants, probably communicating through *Little Fellow*, gave Fraser to understand: we are at war with "the natives of the coast or Islanders," who are very malicious people. If you, strangers, were to go further down the river, Fraser was told, these people will "destroy" you.

The chief who had accompanied the strangers was ready to continue doing so, but "his friends did not approve of his going [and] flocked about him, embracing him with tenderness, as if he was never to return." Accordingly, the chief and his friends declined going further, and so also did *Little Fellow*, saying that "he was afraid of the people at the sea."[93]

---

[92] Howey wrote: "This must have occurred at the mouth of the Coquitlam River, a short distance above the city of New Westminster. No other spot in the vicinity answers this description."

Sage, referring to Simon Fraser at this stage, wrote, "...near the site of New Westminster he met the warlike Cowichans who were none too friendly." I find no evidence in Fraser's narrative that he met any Cowichan people.

[93] Walbran's book says that this tribe is "doubtless the one which is now known as the Cowichan Indians. It is recorded that the Indians of the Lower Fraser were afraid of the 'Ka-way-chin' or 'Indians of the Sea' and therefore put obstacles in Fraser's attempt to reach the main ocean."

Evidently, "the natives of the coast or Islanders" and "the people at the sea" were inhabitants of the river delta who were considered very unfriendly by the people from *Village X*. Fraser was of course extremely anxious to reach the river mouth, and so, despite the warnings and the desertion of *Little Fellow*, he wanted to move along. The locals tried hard to prevent it, but, after much ado, the twenty-four explorers, alone, embarked in the chief's canoe, departed from *Village X*, and continued moving downstream.

ON THE SITE OF PRESENT DAY NEW WESTMINSTER
AND VANCOUVER
(July 2–3, 1808)

<u>July 2:</u>
At about midday, the explorers entered part of the river corresponding to what are now the cities of New Westminster and Vancouver. The following is everything Fraser's narrative says about the time his group spent in this area in separate quotes, (a) to (k), interspersed with my remarks:

a)   We proceeded on for two miles [3.2 km], and came to a place where the river divides into several channels.

Undoubtedly, this was where the river divides into its north and south (main) channels at the eastern end of Lulu Island. Annacis Island lies at the eastern entrance to the south (main) channel.

b)   Seeing a canoe following us we waited for its arrival. One Indian in that canoe embarked with us and conducted us into the right channel.

I refer to him as *Passenger*. The term "the right channel" was undoubtedly meant for the north branch of the Fraser, which the explorers entered from the east, skirting the shore of present-day New Westminster.[94]

c)   In the meantime several Indians from the village followed in canoes, armed with bows and arrows, beating time with their paddles upon the

---

[94] It is interesting that Fraser says he was "conducted" into the north arm. Could it be that his guide wished to avoid Cowichan camps on the south side of Lulu Island?

sides of the canoes, and making signs and gestures highly inimicable[sic]. The one that embarked with us became very unruly singing and dancing, and kicking up the dust.[95]

We threatened him with the effect of our displeasure and he was quiet. This was an alarming crisis, but we were not discouraged: confident of our superiority, at least on the water, we continued.

One can imagine the critical situation. In a long canoe, on the river waters, are twenty-four strangers, provided with firearms, and a local Native man, the Passenger, who bothers them with behaviour they can not understand. The canoe is chased by other canoes, manned by Natives from *Village X*, armed with bows, arrows, clubs, and spears, who show signs of hostility. The strangers are alarmed, but do not panic. They make the Passenger understand that if he keeps misbehaving he will be punished, and he is subdued. They feel safe enough, knowing that while on the water their weapons are superior to those of the chasers, and that they can successfully defend themselves.

d)   At last we came in sight of a gulph or bay of the sea; this the Indians called *Pas-hil-roe*. It runs in a southwest and northwest direction. In this bay are several high and rocky Islands whose summits are covered with snow.

It appears that between quotations (c) and (d), Fraser's narrative skips time and facts, thus leaving something unmentioned. Relating both quotes to quote (g) below, I guess that the men from *Village X* in their canoes, aimed at getting close to Fraser's group, but this group, paddling fast, were able to outdistance their chasers.

By "gulph or bay of the sea" Fraser evidently meant the Strait of Georgia, but it appears from subsequent statements in his narrative that he had no clear idea of the geography of the strait as shown in Vancouver's chart. Presumably, he was not carrying a copy of it.

e)   On the right shore we noticed a village called by the Natives *Misquiame* [nowadays phonetically rendered *Wh'muthkweyum*, *X'muzk'i'um*, etc.]; we directed our course towards it. Our turbulent

---

[95] The phrase "kicking up the dust" intrigued me until I found out its metaphoric meaning in English, obviously intended in this context.

passenger conducted us up a small winding river to a small lake to the village. Here we landed...

At this point, the explorers noted three topographic features. A small winding river which can be identified as Musqueam Creek, which nowadays carries little water. A small lake which presumably only existed during the period of the Fraser's freshet; in any case, it has long disappeared. A village, also now gone, but in an area which is part of the Musqueam Indian Reserve.

The narrative provides only the minimum of details as to how the explorers reached the village, but I surmise that while the tide was high and the canoes from *Village X* were still on the Fraser River, but far behind, the explorers reached the mouth of the small winding river, steered into it, beached the canoe on a tidal mud flat, and then strode into the village. Following the words, "...here we landed," the narrative says:

f) ... and found but a few old men and women; the others fled into the woods upon our approach. The fort is 1500 feet [457 m] in length and 90 feet [27 m] in breadth. The houses, which are constructed as those mentioned in other places, are in rows; besides some that are detached. One of the natives conducted us through all the apartments, and then desired us to go away, as otherwise the Indians would attack us.

From quotes (e) and (f), in which the words "village" and "fort" apply to one and the same place, it appears that it was a fortified village that, for defence purposes, had a rectangular enclosure surrounding the houses, with a total extension of about 13,500 square feet (1250 m^2). Relating these quotations to previous ones, it also appears that the Musqueam inhabitants belonged to "the natives of the coast," or "the people at the sea" that were alleged to be at war with *Village X*, upriver.

g) About this time those that followed us from above arrived. Having spent an hour looking about this place we went to embark, we found the tide had ebbed, and left our canoe on dry land. We had, therefore, to drag it out to the water some distance.

The expression "those that followed us from above" is the basis for some of my guesses concerning the canoes from *Village X*. Here I further guess that while Simon Fraser and some of his companions were visiting the Musqueam village they saw these canoes pushing on, and subsequently arriving nearby. Because Fraser's narrative suggests that the people of the two villages were at war, and it gives no indication that those of *Village X* came ashore, I assume that they remained in their canoes on the river.

h)   The Natives no doubt seeing our difficulty, assumed courage, and began to make their appearance from every direction, in their coats of mail, howling like so many wolves, and brandishing their war clubs.

Which Natives? Fraser's report does not specify clearly enough who they were and what happened next. I assume they were people from the village of Musqueam, and visualize the following sequence of events:

- the explorers left the village and started dragging their long canoe toward the river, while being menaced by the Indians from *Village X*, who were in their canoes;
- while they were doing this, the Musqueam group wearing protective leather coats emerged from the woods and rushed toward the strangers;
- Fraser and his men now found themselves simultaneously threatened by Natives on the river and by Natives ashore, perhaps cooperating, perhaps not;
- with luck, the strangers succeeded in launching the canoe.

i)   At last we got into deep water, and embarked.

Fraser's narrative gives no further details of the fracas. *Passenger* was still with them and as the group ran their canoe downstream, he again began to bother them.

j)   Our turbulent fellow, who [had] embarked in our canoe before, no sooner found himself on board than he began his former impertinences. He asked for our daggers, for our clothes, and in fine for every thing we had. Being convinced of his unfriendly disposition, we turned him out and made him and the others, who were closing in upon us, understand, that if they did not keep their distance we would fire upon them. After this skirmish we continued until we came opposite the second village.

"We turned him out." This was probably easier said than done, and Fraser's report does not explain how this was done without upsetting the canoe.

Although not stated in Fraser's narrative, it seems that the men and canoes from *Village X* remained on the river while the twenty-four voyagers, now without *Passenger*, continued downstream. The term "the second village" rather than "a second village" could suggest that the narrative has a previous reference to this village, but it does not. The second village was a short distance to the west of Musqueam, but exactly where it was and what its name was, are uncertain.[96] I call it for the sake of convenience *Village W*.

k)   Here our curiosity incited us to go ashore; but reflecting upon the reception we experienced at the first [village], and the character of the Natives, it was thought neither prudent nor necessary to run any risk, particularly as we had no provisions, and saw no prospect of procuring any in that hostile quarter. We, therefore, turned our course and with the intention of going back to the friendly Indians for a supply, then to return and prosecute our design. When we came opposite to the hostile village the same fellows who had annoyed us before, advanced to attack us which was echoed by those on shore.

    In this manner they approached so near that we were obliged to adopt a threatening position, and we had to push them off with the muzzles of our guns. Perceiving our determination their courage failed, and they gave up pursuit and crossed to the village.

The explorers, having reached the foreshore of *Village W*, refrained from landing, changed direction, and started heading upstream, aiming to return to the friendly Natives of *Chief's Village*. Surely, the "hostile village" was Musqueam. The rest of the statement is not clear enough, but I surmise the following:

Now Fraser's group in the long canoe were again in the vicinity of Musqueam, where they found themselves again confronted from two directions. On the north shore were villagers, donned in their fighting gear and waving war clubs. On the river were the canoes and men from *Village X* who advanced threateningly toward the strangers. Eventually, after being forcibly fended off, they stopped their threatening advances, and "crossed" to the Musqueam village. Although Fraser had understood that the people of the two villages were

---

[96] Possibly called *Stselax*, but I notice in Bruce Macdonald's book *Vancouver—A Visual History*, pages 10–11 and 12, he shows a camp called *Stsulawh* slightly inland ("upstream") from Musqueam. One map (attributed to Michael Kew) shows a larger village called *Mahli* (*Male*) only a little to the west of Musqueam, but I have no idea if this is what Fraser meant. There were probably also summer camps further west along the south side of the Point Grey peninsula.

antagonists, it seems that Fraser's arrival might have temporarily interrupted their skirmishes.[97]

*****

The twenty-four explorers proceeded to navigate upstream (east) in the large canoe they had borrowed from the Native chief. Fraser's report indicates that at this stage, late on July 2, their intention was to return to the *Chief's Village*, and then with fresh supplies, to come back to the river mouth in order to examine the estuary more closely, and perhaps to visit *Village W*. But this was not to happen.

The visit of Fraser to the areas of what are now the cities of New Westminster and Vancouver was very short and disappointing, perhaps amounting to no more than ten hours altogether. All that he recorded of this interlude is mentioned above. Too little to provide a clear picture of the events, of the villages, and of the Native people he came across.

END OF EXPLORATION

Fraser's report goes on to say:

> The tide was now in our favour, the evening was fine, and we continued our course with great speed until eleven [at night], when we encamped within six miles [10 km] of the chief's village. The men being extremely tired, went to rest; but they were not long in bed before the tide rushed upon the beds and roused them up.

I guess that the spot where the explorers encamped was at a short distance to the east of *Village X*, where Fraser's group had been harassed earlier that day,

---

[97] Some writers have suggested that it was Cowichan people "at the sea" who were hostile, and certainly the journals of Fort Langley attest to frequent marauding by Cowichan war-parties along the Fraser. However, the main Cowichan camp was on the south (main) arm of the river, which Fraser did not visit. Fraser himself suggests that the friction existed between the Kwantlen, who are the westernmost group of the Stó:lō Nation, and the linguistically-close Musqueam of the Vancouver area. Perhaps, in the light of his experience, Fraser assumed wrongly that the Musqueam were the feared "Islanders and natives of the coast" when the Cowichan he did not meet were meant. Then again, perhaps the Kwantlen in their warnings meant all such groups, including people from Nanaimo who also had summer camps along the river.

and that they had now deliberately passed it without stopping, probably taking advantage of the darkness to avoid being noticed by the villagers.

<u>July 3:</u>
> Having been disturbed by the overflowing of the tide, we embarked early and arrived at the chief's village at 5:00 a.m.

Fraser's group were now back at the village whence, two days earlier, they had departed in the chief's large canoe. Here they now encountered *Little Fellow*, who told them that during the intervening time he had been very badly treated by the people of *Village X*. Fraser considered this fact a further indication of danger for his group.

> About this time our Little Fellow, whom we left yesterday at the village below [*Village X?*], made his appearance. He informed us that the Indians after our departure had fixed upon our destruction; that he himself was pillaged, his hands and feet tied, and that they were about to knock him on the head when the chief of the Ackinroe appeared, released him and secured his escape to this place, where he was now detained as a slave.

> Still we were bent upon accomplishing our enterprise to have a sight of the main which was but a short distance from whence we had returned.

Surely, the last paragraph, with the word "main," along with other statements of his quoted above, reveal that, somehow or other, Fraser was aware of the fact that the spot where the river reaches the sea, in the vicinity of *Village W*, was not the "main" sea, the open Pacific, but a "gulph or bay" of it. Perhaps he deduced this from the absence of heavy surf and the sight of the surrounding mountains, or perhaps he had some prior notion of the existence of the Strait of Georgia, of Vancouver Island, and of the Juan de Fuca Strait. Now back at the *Chief's Village*, he still wished to return to the estuary, and thence proceed to the open ocean. Had Fraser truly meant by the "main," the outer coast of Vancouver Island, he could not have been fully aware of how far he was from the entrance of the Juan de Fuca Strait, by sea, over two hundred kilometres away.

For the moment, however, Fraser could do nothing to further this objective because of difficulties, which his journal does not explicit describe, but the essence of which appears to be as follows. Leaving some of his men to watch the large canoe on which they had come, he and other companions went to see the village chief who had lent it. The chief demanded that it be returned to him immediately. Fraser declined to comply. Then the chief invited the men to his house; and they went along with him. Perhaps Fraser was hoping to reach a deal whereby he could continue using that canoe. Suddenly, another one of his men entered the house and reported that some Natives had seized it "and were pillaging our people." Fraser rushed to the scene and "found that some of the Indians from below having arrived had encouraged the others in these violent proceedings." Perhaps these "Indians from below," that is, from a lower part of the river, belonged to *Village X*. Then Fraser faced the offenders with what must have been a masterly histrionic performance:

> I pretended to be in a violent passion, spoke loud, with vehement gestures and signs exactly in their own way; and thus peace and tranquillity were instantly restored.
>
> From these specimens of the insolence and ill nature of the Natives we saw nothing but dangers in our way. We, therefore, relinquished our design and directed our thoughts towards home—but we could not proceed without the canoe, and we had to force it away from the owner leaving a blanket in its place. Thus provided, we pushed off.

Fraser by these means was able to keep the canoe, but he left on the spot something by way of payment in kind to its owner, and, discouraged by the actions of the Natives, gave up his purpose to return to the river mouth. In the meantime, one of his men, afraid of the local people, had been hiding "behind a range of tombs," but now rejoined the group.

The explorers then left the *Chief's Village* and proceeded up the river. They were followed for some time by other canoes manned by local people who were acting in an "unfriendly" and outrageous way, apparently intent on seizing the canoe and upsetting its occupants. However, eventually, the chasers gave up. This must have occurred in the late afternoon or in the evening of July 3.

The party continued upstream toward Fort George, where they arrived on August 6. It had taken Simon Fraser and his companions thirty-five days to reach the river mouth, and thirty-four days to get back to his departure point.

In his narrative, he expressed

> ...great disappointment in not seeing the <u>main ocean</u>, having been so near it as to be almost within view. For we wished very much to

settle the situation by an observation for the longitude.[98] The latitude is 49°N nearly, while that of the entrance of the Columbia is 46°20'N. This River, therefore, is not the Columbia.

It might have been called the Tacoutche River, but, <u>perhaps</u>, soon after Fraser's journey it acquired his name, perhaps bestowed by his colleagues in the North West Company.

*****

This exploration was a wonderful feat, which fully merited a book based on Fraser's narrative, duly revised, enlarged, and illustrated by a map showing the course of the river. It seems that Fraser did indeed wish to publish a book of that kind, but was unable to do so. Surely, he, Stuart, and their fellow-voyagers could have made brave efforts to remember all manner of facts and details about their adventure, and, perhaps with the help of a professional writer and editor, they could have produced a book that would be excellent reading, much more valuable for historical purposes than is the case of Fraser's very meritorious, but somewhat confusing narrative.

A story about Fraser's group

In 1924, the periodical *The Daily Province* published in the city of Vancouver, included an article entitled "Indian Story of Simon Fraser—And How He Barely Escaped Death." Its author was Jason Allard, born in Fort Langley on September 8, 1848. The article says that some years earlier, that is, before 1924, a friend told him the story, as the two "sat together looking across the river at New Westminster." This friend was Staquoisit, nicknamed "Thunder."

The story was that Thunder was young when, in 1808, he witnessed events precipitated by a group of strangers who passed in canoes, along the part of the Fraser River that now belongs to New Westminster and that, in later years, he learned that those strangers were the group led by Simon Fraser and understood some details that had to do with the story: firearms, bagpipes, bugles, pipes, and smoking.

---

[98] This is an interesting comment in that it implies that Stuart carried a chronometer, as did Lewis and Clark, of which there is no previous mention. It is hard to imagine such a sensitive instrument surviving such a journey, yet without one, how could he observe for longitude except by dead-reckoning?

Some of the passages of the story are somewhat unclear, but the essence of it is more or less as follows:

When I was young, my people, the tribe of the *Quo'antle* Indians [Kwantlen], were very powerful, numbered four or five hundred persons, had a winter village where Sapperton [just east of New Westminster] is now, and a summer village camp across the river, where the Liverpool cannery was later located. Besides, we owned Lulu Island.

One day, about thirteen canoes came here, the men in them went ashore and stayed for some time. These men were unlike any of the tribes that lived up the river; they wore strange clothes and some of them had blue eyes. At some time their leader [Fraser], blew a horn, and by means of signs, he let us know that he wanted to go down the river but would come back here. When they started down the river, one of the men put a stick in his mouth and other sticks over his shoulders [bagpipes] and he made funny sounds like music and a bugle was also sounded. Then they continued going down the river. The Musqueam people were at war with another tribe. When they saw the strangers [Fraser and companions] they went out to them, but realizing that they were 'sky people', did not kill them. So Fraser's group went away.

The next day they returned to our village and went ashore. They put sticks in their mouths, took out bags [tobacco] and made fire; then smoke came out of their mouths but the men did not burn, and so we thought that they were supernatural. Fraser fired a musket at a cross made of sticks, and told one of our sub-chiefs, called Quottlekelum, that if he could do the same he would be given the gun. The man tried, but failed.

In the meantime the things that the strangers had in their canoes had become wet; so the strangers spread them out to dry. These things included daggers and ropes. The daggers were of metal and very different from those of our people. In the evening Fraser's group again made music with bagpipes. Then they spent the night here and, in the course of it, our young men stole some of those daggers and ropes. Next morning Fraser's men discovered the theft, searched our people, retrieved the stolen goods, kicked those who had taken them, and then proceeded up river. Among our people it is alright to kick a squaw, but it is bad to kick a brave. The young thieves, feeling offended, wanted to go upriver and kill Fraser's group when they would be camping near Mount Lehman. However, Quottlekelum told them:

143

"Don't kill these strangers, because they have come from above, where the stars are; they took fire into their mouths but did not get burned, and their leader, with that firing instrument, knocked down the cross. This reveals that they have supernatural powers. If you kill them, they will come back with more supernatural power and kill us all."

Heeding the advice, those young men gave up the murderous plan, and Quottlekelum gave them presents so they would not be ashamed any more. [This may have been a standard procedure whereby a chief could solve this kind of embarrassing situation.]

Surely, this story does not concord much with Simon Fraser's report of his adventure. However, it may be based on recollections and tales from Natives who actually saw Fraser's group.

The end of the article suggests that by 1924 the Kwantlen people were reduced to only four or five families. This village must have been one of their villages situated on the north bank of the Fraser, just above New Westminster.

Chapter 10

DAVID THOMPSON'S MAP AND SEQUEL

The explorations effected by Alcalá Galiano on behalf of Spain, and by Vancouver on behalf of Great Britain, produced a fairly accurate chart of the continental coast of the Strait of Georgia. Thus, the coastlines, but only the coastlines, of the area where the city of Vancouver would eventually rise, were drawn in the Galiano chart, first published in 1795, and in a "Chart showing part of the coast of N.W. America" published, along with Vancouver's book, in 1798. Both charts show the estuary of the Columbia River, but give no indication of the Fraser. The continental mainland, what is now the province of British Columbia, remained unknown, though fur traders in the employ of the North West Company were beginning to enter the region.

Fraser's exploration considerably added to the outside world's geographic knowledge of the area. He discovered that the river, because of its rapids and narrow canyon, could not be used for navigation by canoe between its upper levels and the sea. However, on its lower levels, not only canoes, but also large low-keeled vessels could easily navigate for a considerable distance into the river. This part of the river could be used by the company for commercial purposes. On the basis of Fraser's report, of Stuart's records of longitudes and latitudes, and of Vancouver's chart, it was now possible to show the whole course of the river from the Rocky Mountains to its mouth, duly correlated to the pertinent chart of the coast.

One of the North West Company's employees was David Thompson, the man after whom Fraser had named a river. On the company's behalf, Thompson was engaged in exploration, land surveying, and mapping. He became well-informed about the Vancouver chart, and was provided with details obtained by Stewart about the course of the Fraser River. In July 1811, Thompson and seven other men in the Company's service, travelling by canoe, surveyed the Columbia River from Kettle Falls to the spot, near the river mouth, where there was a trading post called Astoria, operated by Americans and Canadians. This exploration completed the dismissal of the erroneous notions formed by Mackenzie and others about this river and the Fraser. On the basis of findings by Fraser and Stuart, Thompson knew approximately the longitude and latitude of the northern mouth of the river they had reconnoitred, the Fraser, and of a village called something like *Misqueame*. A correlation of this data to Vancouver's chart indicated that these features were situated between Point Roberts and Point Grey.

Comparing data, especially longitudes and latitudes, Thompson was able to relate a net of rivers, the Rocky Mountains, Mount Baker, and other topographic features of the mainland territory with its corresponding coast as delineated in Vancouver's chart. During 1813 and 1814, Thompson drew the earliest known piece of trustworthy cartography covering much of the western part of the American continent between latitudes 45°N and 60°N, entitled *Map of the North-West Territory of the Province of Canada from actual survey during the years 1792 to 1812*. Below the title is a note stating that the map marks "the route of Sir Alexander Mackenzie in 1792 down part of the Fraser's River together with the survey of this River to the Pacific Ocean by the late John Stuart."

The map shows a large expanse of territory, the course of a number of rivers, including the Columbia and the Fraser, and also copied from Vancouver's chart, the parts of the Pacific coast where the two rivers meet the sea. Of the Fraser River, it delineates the northern arm of its delta, but not the other arms, and, near its mouth, the map has the inscription *Musquiam Village*, and this remark, "Mr. Simon Fraser and Party returned from the Sortie of the River." On a part that seems to correspond to land, the map has the words "*Pashil Koe*," but a statement in Fraser's narrative, quoted above, implies that "*Pas-hil-roe*" was the Indian name for the Strait of Georgia.

Eventually the manuscript Thompson map was used to produce printed maps. Among the earliest was one by J. Arrowsmith, which mentioned that it was "Compiled from Surveys of Vancouver, Kellet Simpson, Galiano, Valdez, etc." It was printed in London in 1849. Another map, printed in the same city in 1858, shows Vancouver Island and part of the continental territory to the east of it. In the area of what is now Greater Vancouver, the map shows a trail running between Tsawwassen and the confluence of the Fraser and the Pitt Rivers; farther east, it marks and labels Fort Langley, Fort Hope, and Fort Yale.

Originally the map was intended merely for the benefit of the North West Company, and was not published until many years later. However, the fact that canoes, as well as vessels of shallow draft, could easily move up and down the river for a considerable distance along a great valley became widely known. In 1824 James McMillan carried out the reconnaissance of the site of Fort Langley, which in 1827 became the first European settlement in the area (see Appendix 6).

People from overseas began coming to the Lower Mainland and the Fraser Valley, to trade in furs, log, fish, set up trading posts, and to farm, often at times in conflict with the Indigenous inhabitants. Navigating ocean-going vessels into the river, travelling along old trails and cutting new ones, clearing the forest, foreigners began slowly changing the characteristics of the area. When news of the discovery of gold in the Fraser and Thompson Rivers became widely known in the late 1850s, the trickle of immigration became a flood, and royal assent for a new colony, called British Columbia was given shortly after.

Finally, part of Canada

A passage from Fraser's report makes reference to Canada, which he evidently envisaged as a country in the eastern part of North America, not related to the lands of the Rocky Mountains and the west, or to "his" river. In contrast, Thompson's map, along with various documents dating from the first half of the nineteenth century, suggested that, largely because of immigration from Europe, it was the manifest destiny of this region to become part of a Canada under British rule. So it happened, and in the course of time Canada became an independent nation stretching from the Atlantic to the Pacific Oceans.

The Fraser River delta and its vicinity became a large population centre. Its principal city, named after Captain Vancouver, became the terminus of the railway that crosses most of Canada. The province, of which this area forms part, was officially named after the Columbia River district of the fur-trading era. There are islands named after Vancouver, Galiano, and Valdés, and a University named after Fraser. Vancouver city has streets named after Narváez and Broughton. A part of Burrard Inlet is called Spanish Banks,[99] and there is a Langara golf course. The street called Blanca was apparently so named in memory of the *Boca de Florida Blanca*. These and other features are reminders of the explorations effected by Narváez, Vancouver, Galiano, Valdés, and Fraser, and the men that laboured under their leadership.

The proto-Vancouverite

As mentioned in Chapter 6 and in the Appendices of this work, the Alcalá Galiano expedition understood that *Sasamat* was the name that local inhabitants applied to Burrard Inlet, an inlet that is a big part of why the city of Vancouver is here today.

For the First Nations people, this was their land and their home, and the early explorers from Europe met a number of them, although none of their names are mentioned in the records. Among these people was the Chief of Point Grey whose portrait was sketched by José Cardero in 1792. As no other Native person of the area was identified and portrayed before, this chief may be considered to be the earliest known Vancouverite.

Because his own name was not recorded, I suggest, albeit capriciously, that he be nicknamed "Chief Sasamat." Furthermore, I suggest that, in honour of the First Nations people of this site, this chief be commemorated, that the municipal authorities publicise his portrait and give him a title, such as *The City Father* or *The First Vancouverite*.

---

[99] Some publications have statements to the effect that the schooners *Sutil* and *Mexicana* were anchored just off those banks, which evidently was not the case.

SELECTED BIBLIOGRAPHY

ALLEN, RICHARD EDWARD. *Origin of Street and Place Names. A Pictorial History of Vancouver: Book 1.* Winnipeg, Josten's, 1982.

[BELL, EDWARD] supposed author. *A New Vancouver Journal on the Discovery of Puget Sound, by a Member of the Chatham's Crew*; edited by Edmond S. Meany. Seattle, Wash., University of Washington, 1915. (Attributed to Edward Bell, clerk of the ship Chatham.)

BRITISH COLUMBIA. AGENT GENERAL IN LONDON. British Columbia; information for emigrants. London, Printed by Wm Clowes & Son, 1873.

CAMPBELL, MARJORIE WILKINS. *The Savage River; seventy-one days with Simon Fraser.* Toronto, Macmillan, 1968.

DOE, NICHOLAS. "Some Anomalies in a Spanish Chart of Vancouver Island 1791." *Lighthouse*, Journal of the Canadian Hydrographic Association, No. 56, Fall 1997.

ELLIOTT, T.C. "Journal of John Work, November and December 1824." *Washington Historical Quarterly*, Vol. 3, No. 3, July 1912.

ESPINOSA Y TELLO, JOSE. *Relación del viage hecho por las goletas Sutil y Mexicana, en el año de 1792, para reconocer el estrecho de Fuca.* Madrid, Imprenta Real, 1802.

FRASER, SIMON. "Journal of a Voyage from the Rocky Mountains to the Pacific Coast, 1808," in L.F.R. Masson, *Les Bourgeois de la Compagnie du Nord-ouest.* Quebec, A. Coté, 1889.

FRASER, SIMON. *Letters and journals, 1806-1808*. Edited by W. Kaye Lamb. Toronto, Macmillan, 1960.

HIGUERAS RODRIGUEZ, MARIA DOLORES. *Catálogo Critico de los Documentos de la Expedición Malaspina (1789-1794) del Museo Naval*. Madrid, Museo Naval, 1985.

HOWAY, F.W. "The Search for the Fraser by Sea and Land." in *Historical Papers*, Art, Historical and Scientific Association, Vancouver, 1908.

HUTCHISON, BRUCE. *The Fraser*. Toronto, Clarke, Irwin, 1950. (Rivers of America.)

KING, JANE, ed. *British Columbia Handbook*, 3rd ed. Chico, Calif., Moon Publications, 1994.

KENDRICK, JOHN, ed. *The Voyage of Sutil and Mexicana, 1792*. Translated, and with an introduction by John Kendrick. Spokane, Wash., The Arthur Clark Company, 1991.

MACDONALD, BRUCE. *Vancouver; a Visual History*. Vancouver, Talonbooks, 1992.

MANBY, THOMAS. *Journal of Vancouver's Voyage, 1790-1793*. Manuscript in the William Robertson Coe Collection, Yale University Library. University of British Columbia has a copy.

MATTHEWS, JAMES SKITT. "Pilot Commander Don José María Narváez, 1791." *Vancouver Historical Journal*, Vol. 4, 1961.

MEANEY, EDMOND S., ed. *Vancouver's Discovery of Puget Sound*. Portland, Binfords & Mort, 1957.

MENZIES, ARCHIBALD. *Menzies' Journal of Vancouver's Voyage, April to October 1792*; ed. by C.F. Newcombe. Victoria, W.H. Cullin, 1923.

MENZIES, ARCHIBALD. [Private Journal] Add. Ms. 32641, British Library, London, England.

NAISH, JOHN M. *The Interwoven Lives of George Vancouver, Archibald Menzies, Joseph Whidbey, and Peter Puget: exploring the Pacific Northwest Coast.* Lewiston, N.Y., Edwin Mellen Press, 1996.

ROBERTS, JOHN E. "A Discovery Journal," unpublished manuscript. Victoria, B.C., 1996.

SAGE, WALTER. "Simon Fraser Explorer and Fur Trader," in *Proceedings* of the Pacific Coast Branch of the American Historical Association, 1929.

SANCHEZ, JOSEPH P. *Spanish Bluecoats; the Catalonian Volunteers in Northwestern New Spain, 1767-1810.* Albuquerque, University of New Mexico Press, 1990.

SUTTLES, WAYNE, ed. *Handbook of North American Indians*, Vol. 7, Northwest Coast. Washington, Smithsonian Institution, 1990.

VANCOUVER, GEORGE. *A Voyage of Discovery to the North Pacific Ocean, and Round the World.* London, 1798. (3 volumes and atlas)

VANCOUVER, GEORGE. *A Voyage...* A new edition, with corrections. London, 1801. (6 volumes)

VANCOUVER, GEORGE. *A Voyage... 1791-1795*, edited by W. Kaye Lamb. London, The Hakluyt Society, 1984. (3 volumes) (This has the whole text of Vancouver's Voyage, with a detailed introduction and many notes.)

The Vancouver Island Pilot, containing Sailing Directions for the Coasts of Vancouver Island, and part of British Columbia. London, Hydrographic Office, 1864.

WAGNER, HENRY RAUP. Spanish Explorations in the Strait of Juan de Fuca. Santa Ana, Calif., Fine Arts Press, 1933. (This work includes English translations of most of the original reports about the Eliza and the Galiano expeditions, with helpful indices.)

WALBRAN, JOHN T. *British Columbia Coast Names.* Ottawa, Government Printing Bureau, 1909.

Appendix 1

QUOTATIONS FROM SPANISH MANUSCRIPTS
(abbreviated words spelled in full)

FROM THE ELIZA EXPEDITION

Museo Naval, Madrid, Ms. 331, fol. 23.

Passage regarding *Canal de Nuestra Señora del Rosario la Marinera* (Strait of Georgia), from a report by the officer Juan Pantoja.

En el Norte y Sur tiene barias bocas, que tampoco se pudieron reconoser, y en lo que registraron de una y otra se encuentran barios Rios de Agua dulce y en la primera se consive haver alguno sumamente caudaloso, por que proximo a la Isla de Zepeda y en distancia de 2 leguas navegaron sobre una linea de Agua blanca mas dulce que salobre, y en una y otra costa hay buenos surgideros, muchas porciones de tierra llana, la misma abundancia de pastos y Quadrupedos que en el mencionado Estrecho [de Juan de Fuca] y en la Isla de Zepeda increible abundancia de ricos salmones y numerosa Indiada mucho mas dociles y tratables que los de la entrada, quienes hablan enteramente distinto Ydioma, y sin embargo de no entenderles la Lengua expresaron con bastante claridad haver muy adentro del Canal Embarcaciones mas grandes que la Goleta [Santa Saturnina] y uno de ellos traia unas Manillas (que no quiso cambiar) de laton muy fino, grabadas al parecer con Buril, cosa que no se ha visto en ninguno de los Yndios de toda la Costa, ni menos en las Bugerias que han taido los Buques Extranjeros que han estado en Noca [Nootka] desde que nosotros lo conocimos.

FROM THE GALIANO EXPEDITION

Archivo General de la Nación, Mexico City, Section Provincias Internas, Vol. 134, f. 418-431. E 27c.

Passage from the report by Alcalá Galiano and Cayetano Valdés that I call *Extracto*. It concerns events of the early hours of June 13, 1792, when these officers reconnoitred Boundary Bay and found that, contrary to what the Eliza chart had suggested, there was no southern access to the supposed *Boca de Floridablanca*. As a consequence of this finding, Boundary Bay in the Galiano charts is called *Ensenada del Engaño*, that is, Bay of Deception.

> *Nuestro obgeto era amanecer a la boca del Canal de Floridablanca,*
> *e internar con el...pero a la madrugada nos hallamos en poca agua,y*
> *no hallando el Canal en varios bordos que dimos fondeamos, y con el*
> *bote sondamos hasta una braza proximo a la Costa: quando amanecio*
> *el 13 nos vimos en una ensenada cerrada con arboleda al redor donde*
> *la maior agua es de 4 1/2 brazas conocimos que la que se llamó Ysla*
> *de Zepeda, y efectivamente lo parecia no lo era, y que para entrar en*
> *el Canal seria preciso ir por el N. de las Yslas de Lángara para esto*
> *dimos la vela, y bordeamos con los Escandallos en la mano.*

Museo Naval, Madrid, Ms. 144, fol. 497.

Passage written in the first person singular but with no specification as to who was the author. The first paragraph refers to contact of the Galiano expedition with Natives in the vicinity of "the Langara islands", that is Point Grey. The second paragraph begins with a reference to Burrard Inlet in general, and mentions that the Native people called it *Sasamat*, and goes on to describe the explorations of a party led by the officers Vernacci and Salamanca.

> *Estando fondeados cerca del fronton de la Punta N.O. de las Islas de*
> *Lángara vinieron a bordo varas canoas de lo interior algunas de ellas*
> *hasta con 9 hombres: pero aunque estos eran vivos e indicaban tener*
> *bastante comprehension no hallaba yo en ellos tanta gracia e*

intrepidez que en los antecedentes: tambien venian armados y trahian sus utiles de pesca, entre ellos unas redes pequeñas pero bien hechas.

En el canal llamado por los nuestros de Florida Blanca y por los naturales Sasamat se encuentran pocos abitantes. A la entrada he visto dos Rancherias y varios Indios de ellas atracaron con sus canoas a nuestros botes, nos regalaron pescado, y manifestaron complacencia a tratar con nosotros. Sus vestidos, armas etc. eran mui semejantes en todo a las de los que haviamos tratado antes: si no me parecieron tan robustos y abiles como los que haviamos visto venir de hacia la Isla de Cepeda. No volvimos a ver otros en [100] todo lo restante de nuestra navegacion por el brazo E. pero cuando acabamos el del N. en la orillas del Rio en que finaliza el canal vimos una pequeña rancheria de que huyeron immediatamente las mujeres que nos divisaron. Algunos de los Indios se embarcaron en sus canoas y se acercaron a nosotros en particular un mozo que parecia el tays,[101] que mandaba y era obedecido de los Indios de un modo que antes [yo] no havia reparado en otros parajes. Venian mas cuviertos con mantas que los de la entrada pero estas eran iguales a las de aquellos. Despues de haber estado un rato con nosotros se interiorisaron en el rio saltaron en tierra y se metieron en el Bosque llebando sus armas.

WATER: SWEET OR BRACKISH?
With reference to Chapter 7, page 98

Two Statements about Water

These statements do not lend themselves to literal translations. Following are the statements and accurate renderings of what they mean.

---

[100] Here the manuscript has the word *la* and the unfinished word *dir*. They should be overlooked, as the sentence is perfectly clear without them.

[101] *Tays* is a Nootkan word that means chief and that in English documents is generally spelled *tayee*.

Museo Naval, Madrid, Ms. 143, fol. 191v.

1)   *haviendo notado un Marinero que le faltavan unos calzones que estaban enjugandose con ropa que la abundancia de agua dulce habia proporcionado a nuestra gente el labar.*

MEANING: ...a sailor, having noticed the disappearance of his breeches [pants] which were drying, along with other clothing which the abundance of fresh water had enabled our people to wash.

M. Naval, Madrid, Ms. 619, fol. 61r.

2)   *...por haber faltado unos calzones de un Marinero que estaban enjugandose porque con la proporcion del Agua Salobre, todos habian labado su ropa.*

MEANING: ... after the disappearance of the breeches of one of the sailors, which were drying because, with the availability of brackish water, all had washed their clothes.

Another manuscript has the same statement.

Appendix 2

ANCHORAGE OF *SUTIL* AND *MEXICANA* OFF POINT GREY

Alcalá Galiano's narrative in its entry for June 20, 1792 says:

> The wind remained nearly calm, and we advanced very slowly, sounding continuously with a 70 fathom line. We found no bottom until we suddenly hit 25 fathoms, and immediately afterwards 15 fathoms. We manoeuvred to drop anchor, which was promptly done, in 10 fathoms. We let the anchor go at that depth, taking a bearing from our anchorage to the northerly part of the *Punta de Lángara* [Point Grey] at E5°N and to the middle of one of the rounded islands which are in the *Bocas del Carmelo* [entrance to Howe Sound] at N5°E.

Nicholas Doe of White Rock, B.C., explains this point as follows:

> The Eliza chart of 1791, *Carta que comprehende...*, incorrectly shows both Point Grey and Point Roberts as islands. Point Roberts was identified as *Isla de Zepeda* (Zepeda Island), and Point Grey as either a single island, or in some copies, as belonging to a group of islands called *Isla(s) de Lángara* (Langara Island[s]). If several islands were meant, the Langara group probably included Sea Island, which the Eliza chart appears to show in its entirety, and maybe also Lulu Island, and Westham Island to the south, although only the outer coasts of these are depicted.
>
> Significantly, two tiny anchors have been drawn a short distance to the west of Point Grey. These are cartographic symbols for a "good anchorage" and probably indicate that the schooner *Santa Saturnina*

and its accompanying longboat stopped there for a while during the exploration of the Strait of Georgia in July 1791.

When the Galiano and Valdés expedition arrived in 1792 to continue the explorations, it was quickly realised that Point Grey and Point Roberts were not in fact islands, and they were consequently renamed *Punta de Lángara* (Langara Point) and *Punta de Zepeda* (Zepeda Point) respectively.

A manuscript draft of the Galiano report, in a passage describing the events of June 19, 1792, has the statement (not included in other documents):

Desde las 9 empezamos a sondar con 40 brazas procurando hallar el ancladero que nos ofrecia la Carta.

From nine o'clock we began to sound on 40 fathoms, trying to find the anchorage that the chart was offering us.

This statement clearly suggests that Galiano and Valdés had a copy of the Eliza chart and were attempting to find the location indicated by the two anchor symbols.

The draft of Galiano's report and the book *Relación* give consistent accounts of the attempts to find the anchorage. The two vessels first dropped anchor at about 3:30 a.m. June 20 somewhere between Point Grey and Point Roberts from which, according to the accounts, Point Grey bore N15°W, and Point Roberts S49°E. Realizing that this was not a safe position on account of the shallowness of the water, they bore away SSW until they were well clear of the mud flats, then headed NNW until they reached the latitude of Point Grey.[102] From there they worked their way to the second anchorage as described in Alcalá Galiano's narrative for June 20, 1792 quoted at the head of this Appendix.

Unfortunately, none of the bearings given in the account enable the two anchorages to be located in a straightforward manner. It is clear from the 1792 chart of the Galiano expedition that, possibly as a result of errors in the determinations of latitude and longitude, or of compass

---

[102] SSW with respect to magnetic north would correspond to a true bearing of SW, and NNW magnetic to approximately N true.

deviation, the cartographers have shown the region between Point Grey and Point Roberts rotated counter-clockwise from true north by 15°. This is the sort of error that also arises when a sketch oriented to magnetic (compass) north is transcribed, <u>without rotation</u>, to a chart oriented to true (geographic) north. A similar kind of error occurs in the Eliza chart.

The second of the two anchorages is best located from the fact that it was in ten fathoms of water and that the difference in the bearings of the northerly part of Point Grey E5°N (85°) and the island in the mouth of Howe Sound N5°E (5°) was 80°. This approach avoids having to know what Galiano considered to be the variation of the compass, which was in fact roughly 19°E in English Bay in 1792.

Assuming that Galiano's fathoms (*brazas*) are only slightly smaller than modern fathoms,[103] then on a modern chart (3311) they must have been at 49°16.3'N, 123°17.1'W, about 1.7 km due west of the present base of the cliff at Point Grey. I say "present" because the cliff is eroding quite rapidly. The more northerly of the two anchor symbols on the Eliza chart of 1791 is practically at this location and the depth is marked as ten fathoms.

The small rounded island in Howe Sound is almost certainly Passage Island which bears 351° (true) from this anchorage. The alternative identification is Mount Gardner on Bowen Island, 327°(true); however, while Passage Island can be fairly described as "rounded," Bowen Island with its three high points can not.

From the second anchorage, the northernmost point of Point Grey would be seen at about 71° (true), which is 80° to the east of Passage Island as required by Galiano's statement. Evidently the two bearings in the accounts, taken as true bearings, are 14° too far clockwise. As magnetic bearings they would be about 33° too far clockwise, which is too large to be likely.

The bearings given for the first anchorage, N15°W (345°) and S49°E (131°), taken as true bearings, and plotted on a modern chart

---

[103] Nowadays, ten fathoms is reckoned as being sixty feet (18.3 m), but Galiano's reckoning was probably nearer 16.7 m. The ships' draft was roughly a fathom (1.8 m).

(3463), puts the anchorage at about 49°01'N, 123°10'W, which is close to the present-day coal terminal on the south end of Roberts Bank. This is a little too far south to be credible. Rotating the bearings for the anchorage 14° counter-clockwise, as is suggested is needed by the analysis above, unfortunately only produces a nonsensical result. However, rotating them 15° clockwise, thereby introducing exactly the same error as in Galiano's chart, makes perfect sense. Bearings of N (0°) and S34°E (146°), instead of N15°W (345°) and S49°E (131°), put the anchorage on the edge of Sturgeon Bank at 49°09'N, 123°16'W. This is north of Westham Island and close to the south arm of the Fraser off Steveston, at the north end of a series of shallow soundings on Galiano's chart.[104]

If this is the true position of the anchorage, the Spanish captains showed good judgment in leaving when they did as they had arrived only a day after a new moon and at the height of a spring tide.[105] By noon, the water was three metres lower and they may well have been stranded had they remained where they were.

---

[104] The water at the anchorage was only 2.5 fathoms (*brazas*) or about 4.2 m deep.

[105] The tides at the mouth of the Fraser River on June 20, 1792 were:

HLW	3.4 m	00:15 a.m.
LHW	3.8 m	04:02 a.m.
LLW	0.5 m	11:33 a.m.
HHW	4.5 m	07:15 p.m., local apparent time.

Appendix 3

REGARDING COUNT FLORIDABLANCA, TOPONYMS, AND PLATES 4 to 13

The Eliza exploration of 1791 occurred at a time when seafaring European nations, particularly Spain and Great Britain, were intensely interested in the geography of the Northwest Coast. At the time, it was not known if somewhere along this complex coastline there might be the entrance to a passage that would eventually lead from the Pacific to the Atlantic Ocean. The "discovery" of a broad opening on the continental coast of the Pacific, could do nothing but encourage the belief that there was such a navigable passage. The Eliza chart shows such an opening at latitude 49°30'N, and names it *Boca de Florida Blanca*. This was an imaginary feature, the existence of which was a consequence of the faulty cartography of Narváez and Verdía, and their misunderstanding of the lie of the land. Of course, it is possible that one or both of these men considered it to be a very important feature. It must have been from a sketch by Narváez, that the feature came to be incorporated in the Eliza chart. Yet, curiously, the existing written records of their exploration, the reports of Eliza, Pantoja, and Carrasco, contain not a single reference to this *boca*.[106]

In a rough copy of the Eliza chart included in Pantoja's report, this feature is labelled *Boca de la Bodega*, after the then commander of the naval base at San Blas, Juan Francisco de la Bodega y Quadra. In other copies of the Eliza chart, obviously drawn at a later date, the feature is labelled after Count Floridablanca (one word, not two) who, at the time, was the principal minister to the King of Spain, a position somewhat similar to that of Prime Minister in

---

[106] This misconception appears in the book *Relación* and in at least one book of recent times.

Great Britain. That is, a change was made that bestowed on the imaginary *boca* the name of the person in the Spanish government, whose power was second only to that of the king. This merits the assumption that the non-existent *boca* was assumed by somebody to be a very important feature, despite its not having been mentioned in Eliza's report.

When in 1792, the Alcalá Galiano expedition found that there was no such *boca*, it applied the name *Brazo de Florida Blanca* to the whole of Burrard Inlet. So named, it appeared in the Galiano chart published in 1795, what I call Galiano Map 2 (Plate 12).

Nevertheless, there are curious anomalies. The book *Relación*, published in 1802, makes some references to *Boca de Floridablanca* (Floridablanca mouth) and reports that Galiano and Valdés found that there was no such feature. Yet, in subsequent pages, the book designates Burrard Inlet as *Canal de Floridablanca*. The atlas of the same date, 1802, a companion of the book, includes what I call Galiano Map 3 (Plate 13), which is very similar to the one of 1795 except for a few changes in toponymy. One of the changes made was to label Burrard Inlet as *Canal de Sasamat*. So although the book reports that the Galiano expedition reconnoitred the *Canal de Floridablanca*, no such denomination appears in the atlas. There is nothing in either the book or the atlas to explain this discrepancy. Nor have I found any documents of that period which provide an explanation the above anomalies. I suggest the following.

On February 28, 1792, while the Galiano expedition was preparing to sail from Acapulco for its exploratory assignment, Count Floridablanca was summarily dismissed from his post as the principal minister of the King of Spain. Galiano had no chance of knowing this until after his voyage had been completed. For several years thereafter, Floridablanca was ostracised and disregarded by the Spanish government. Yet, in 1795, three years after his dismissal, the chart I call Galiano Map 2 was published, retaining Floridablanca's name for Burrard Inlet. Not until the chart of 1802 (Galiano Map 3) was published, was this inlet designated as *Canal de Sasamat*. Probably what happened was that orders were given to the publishers of the atlas to remove the name of the disgraced minister, and the publishers then gave to the *Canal* the name *Sasamat*, which the Galiano expedition had understood was the Native people's name for the inlet. However, for some reason, possibly carelessness, this editing change was not also made to the corresponding text of the book *Relación*.

Possibly other editing changes were made concerning the name for what is now called Boundary Bay, for although the atlas names it *Ensenada del Engaño* (Deception Bay), no such name appears in the accompanying book.

In summary:

Boca de la Bodega appears in a rough sketch by Pantoja (1791), but not in any of the original reports;

Boca de Floridablanca appears in a final version of the Eliza chart, but not in any of the original reports. The name occurs again in the 1802 publication, but only in text to the effect that it does not exist;

Brazo de Floridablanca appears in Galiano's records (1792), report and chart (published 1795);

Canal de Floridablanca appears in the 1802 publication, but only in the text. Presumably the editors should have changed it to the name below, but neglected to do so;

Canal de Sasamat appears in the 1802 publication, but only in the chart.

Ensenada del Engaño appears in the 1802 publication, but only in the chart.

Appendix 4

REGARDING *SASAMAT*
(mentioned in Chapter 7 and Appendix 3)

The records of the Alcalá Galiano expedition include a statement to the effect that what is now known as Burrard Inlet, was called *Sasamat* by the local inhabitants, and *Canal de Floridablanca* by the Spaniards. The book *Relación*, page 69, contains the phrase: "The northern branch of the Canal that we call after Floridablanca and the Natives call *Sasamat* ends in a river..." The same book has a list of Native toponyms together with the corresponding ones given by the Spaniards. The list includes *Boca de Floridablanca—Sasamat*. These passages of the book are translated in Wagner's book on the exploration of the Juan de Fuca Strait. As mentioned in Appendix 3, the Spanish chart published in 1802 clearly designates the whole of Burrard Inlet as *Canal de Sasamat*, but it is not at all clear when and how the Spanish expedition of 1792 heard this name.

In 1957, the then mayor of North Vancouver, Charles W. Cates, wrote to the head of the Naval Museum in Madrid a letter dated April 16, 1957,[107] that included this paragraph:

I thought of you and your famous explorers of the *Canal de Sasamat*.

Incidentally, I speak a good deal of our local Indian language and have always felt that Dons Galiano and Valdés misunderstood the word when they referred to 'Sasamat'. I have checked very carefully and have finally reached the solution that what the Indians really did reply when asked as to where they lived was *Tslaylwut-h* [*Tsleil Waututh*], which means 'inside', and in their very soft form of speech,

---

[107] I found Mayor Cates' letter in the Naval Museum of Madrid, among documents on the Spanish explorations.

your people no doubt thought they said *Sasamat*. There is no doubt of this mistake, because in your explorers' log of the event they refer to the river at the head of the inlet as *Sasamat*, whereas the Indian name for it to-day is *Tslaylwut-h*.

Mayor Cates' reference to "your explorers' log of the event" (slightly inaccurate) is evidently a reference from Wagner's book. The mayor may well have been right in asserting that the Native name for the river that flows into the head of Indian Arm was *Tslaylwut-h*; however, his conclusion that the Spaniards <u>wrote</u> the name *Sasamat* on hearing the Natives of Indian Arm <u>pronounce</u> the name *Tslaylwut-h* is unconvincing. Neither the vowels nor the consonants of the two words tally well with one another. Still, the mayor deserves much credit for his interest in the matter.

The book *A Pictorial History of Vancouver: Book 1, Origin of Street and Place Names*, by Richard Edward Allen, published in 1982, page 126, says that the Spanish officers Vernaci and Salamanca, during their exploration of the head of Indian Arm "met a few Indians whom they mistakenly named *Sasamat*—the name has not been claimed by any local tribe." The first part of this statement is inaccurate, but the second part is interesting in that it suggests that the First Nations people living in Burrard Inlet in recent times do not know the name or word "Sasamat." The Smithsonian "Handbook of North American Indians," Volume 7, gives the name of the Indian Arm Indians in the 19th century as *Saleelwat* which admittedly does bear some resemblance to *Sasamat*, but when this name first came into use is hard to establish.[108]

In any case, the Spanish records do not warrant the conclusion that the Spaniards understood *Sasamat* to be either the name of the river or of an Indian Band; those records clearly reveal that the Alcalá Galiano expedition understood, rightly or wrongly, that *Sasamat* was the Native name for <u>the whole</u> of Burrard Inlet.

Although there appears to be little chance of solving the mystery of the origin of this word, it has gained recognition since it is now applied to a lake located near Indian Arm, and to a short street in the Point Grey section of the city of Vancouver.

---

[108] Other 19th-century names are *Selilwet* for the Indian River, and *Selilwetolth* for Indian Arm. These names are given in J.E.(Ted) Robert's book *A Discovery Journal*.

Appendix 5

INDIAN BOY, INTERTRIBAL TRADE, ETC.

This Appendix contains a note on certain parts of the records of the Eliza expedition which, although not directly pertinent to the main topic, are of interest because they have been wrongly suggested as having to do with the Vancouver area.

There is some evidence that Europeans who visited the Northwest Coast of America in the second half of the eighteenth century made contact with adult Natives who offered children for sale, and that some children were purchased by sailors of various nationalities.

A number of purchases were effected by crews of Spanish vessels between 1789 and 1792. Practically all the youngsters were taken to the port of Monterey in California, then under Spanish dominion, or to San Blas in what is now Mexico, where they were placed in the care of tutors. It is very unlikely that any of them ever returned to their original home. The Spanish authorities disapproved of these acquisitions, and the practice was stopped after 1792.

Acquisitions of this kind were made in 1791 by the expedition led by Francisco de Eliza, whose report says, "during the stay at Clayoucuat and in the Strait, seven Indian girls and thirteen Indian boys whose ages range from 4 to 12 years, were bought for copper sheets." The report adds that expedition members such as officers, caulkers, carpenters, and gunners took care of these children, in order to educate and teach them.[109]

---

[109] Eliza's report, last paragraph. The report mentions that on July 25, while the Expedition was still at Discovery Bay (*Puerto de Quadra*), he, Eliza, decided that it would return to Nootka. The reason? "*...por hallarme con nueve enfermos, no tener dietas que darles y ademas empezar a picarse de escorbuto algunos de la tripulacion.*" This means: because of finding myself with

Evidently, the words Clayoucuat and "the Strait" refer to Clayoquot Sound and the Juan de Fuca Strait. Pantoja's report includes a very similar statement. Both statements clearly imply that these purchases, or adoptions, of children were made at one or more of the places where the expedition's two vessels "stayed" for some time.

Pantoja's report also contains the following paragraph, which, in all probability, refers to one of these twenty children:

> ...se ha savido por un niño de edad de 11 o 12 años que rescato el Despensero Jose Ignacio Gonzalez, que en la Costa del Norte hay tierras llanas y que por ellas bienen [vienen] y tardan dos Lunas, mucha gente al Comercio del Pescado trayendo fierro Cobre y Abalorios azules los que usan distinta vestimenta, arcos y flechas uno y otro mayor que los suyos y unos animales Grandes quadrupedos con la Pesuña redonda y Clin y Cola larga y que a estos les arman sobre el Lomo 4 tercios de Pescado y para que caminen los azotan con un Cuero, y comprendiendosele por las señas serian Cavallos se le mostro uno pintado y luego que lo vido dijo que asi eran.[110]

The wording of this statement is somewhat awkward, but the following is a correct and nearly literal translation:

> ...a boy of eleven or twelve years of age who was ransomed by the storekeeper José Ignacio González, was understood to state that on the Northern Coast there are flat lands, and that through these lands many people come to trade for fish, effecting trips that take them two months. They bring iron, copper, and blue beads. They differ from his own people in dress and in having bigger bows and arrows. They

---

nine men ill, not having [food] rations to give them, and, furthermore, scurvy beginning to hit [afflict] some of the crew.

The comment on rations could hardly have been exactly true, but obviously indicated a shortage of food. Yet, it is after this statement that the report has the 52 words about the acquisition of twenty children. Eliza had them on board *San Carlos*, during its trip from the Juan de Fuca Strait to Nootka, where it arrived on August 30; surely, these children must have been fed with at least some of those rations.

[110] Pantoja's report, fol. 241. Another passage of the report has a statement similar to the one by Eliza quoted in this Appendix.

travel with large quadruped animals that have round hooves and long manes and tails. These people load 4 *tercios* of fish on the backs of these animals, and whip them with a piece of leather to make them walk. We [the Spaniards] assuming from his expressions and mimicry that these animals were horses, showed the boy a drawing of one, and when he saw it, he said that such were those animals.[111]

In this statement the word *vienen*, meaning come, is not qualified by any other expression that might answer the obvious question: come here? Unfortunately, this the only record of the boy and his story.

Henry R. Wagner's book on the Spanish explorations of the Juan de Fuca Strait, and a few other publications of more recent times, contain comments to the effect that this story has a ring of truth. It may be so, but, of course, it is possible that what the boy actually said was not exactly or totally conveyed by Pantoja.

From the context of the data on this and other cases of the trade with children, it is obvious that the boy was purveyed by some adult Natives who had been keeping him. His story raises questions.

Questions

Does it fit with what is known, or is practically certain, about what were then realities of the area of Vancouver Island, the Juan de Fuca Strait, and the corresponding parts of the continental mainland?

Where was the boy acquired? Did his people reside in this region, or was he from elsewhere? How did he communicate his story when there was an obvious language barrier to be overcome?

---

[111] The words *dos Lunas* mean two moons or months. The word *tardan* is from the verb *tardar*, which has no exact English equivalent; it means length of time, the time spent in some action. The word *tercios* is a unit of weight whose equivalent in kilograms is not clear. The expression *por las señas* clearly suggests help to comprehension by means of mimicry and gesticulation. The word *clin* is a misspelling for *crin*. The meaning of the word *pintado* is "painted," but in this case it probably refers to a drawing, either original or in print.

The fact that Pantoja referred to these boys as being ransomed suggests that he assumed they had been kidnapped. This is possible, or they might have been the children of slaves.

Considerations

By sea, as well as through rivers, lakes and land, a variety of articles such as glass beads and pieces of metal, originating in other parts of the world, reached Native American people, including those that lived in the region between the Rocky Mountains and the Pacific Coast. Some such articles exchanged hands in intertribal barter, and some came to be owned by Natives along the banks of the Fraser River, as witnessed by Simon Fraser.

Natives of the Northwest Coast, in general, were eager to obtain copper sheets.

There were trails across the land west of the Rocky Mountains. Such was the case along lands through which the Fraser River flows. A trail between Pemberton and Squamish, which was explored in 1856 by J.W. McKay, may well have already been in existence in 1791.

There were no horses on Vancouver Island or on the other islands of the region, but there were Native peoples who used domesticated horses in parts of the continent west of the Rocky Mountains visited by Simon Fraser, Alexander Henry, and David Thompson early in the eighteenth century. There is substantial evidence of this in Fraser's narrative describing his exploration of the river now named after him.

The story tells of people with horses taking round trips for the purpose of obtaining fish to take back home. If this is true, it must have been smoked or dried fish. There is ample evidence that the inhabitants of the Northwest Coast, both on the continental mainland and on the islands, were accustomed to drying and smoking fish, and to keeping supplies of it for the periods of the year when they did little or no fishing.

It seems obvious that the boy made the statement at the place where he was acquired by González, which could only be one of the places where one or more of the expedition's three vessels tarried for some time. The packetboat *San Carlos* tarried at four places. For about fourteen days it was at Clayoquot Sound on the west side of Vancouver Island; for thirty days at Esquimalt Bay on the southeastern tip of Vancouver Island; for thirty-three days at Port Discovery on the southeastern side of the Juan de Fuca Strait; and for four days at Neah Bay at the southern entrance of the Juan de Fuca Strait. The schooner *Santa Saturnina* and the longboat spent some time at each of these places, and, in the course of their exploratory trips, they stopped briefly at other places that are indicated with anchors on the Eliza chart.

Eliza's statement reveals that José Ignacio González held the position of storekeeper, that is, safekeeper and distributor of edibles, beverages, and many other articles. I suppose that this job had to do with the whole of the expedition; it was centred in its principal vessel, the *San Carlos*, on which he served for the whole of the time. I doubt there was a specific storekeeper for the *Santa Saturnina*, even less likely for the longboat while they were engaged in exploration, because the number of men serving in them was small, and they carried supplies of food and water for no more than twenty days. Thus, I conjecture that González was always aboard the *San Carlos*, and that he adopted the boy at one of the four bays or ports where it tarried for several days.

Which of those four places were accessible to humans travelling with horses? Neither Clayoquot Sound nor Esquimalt Bay, because they are on Vancouver Island. Neah Bay and Discovery Bay were probably accessible, but not from some contiguous land far away to the north.

What then? Perhaps the boy did not mean that people with horses travelled precisely to the bay where the Eliza expedition acquired him, but to the place where his own people dwelt, which may have been elsewhere. In other words: perhaps his people lived at some other place, whence they brought him to the place where part, or the whole, of the Eliza expedition was staying at the time. The following are some points relevant to the question.

In 1790, navigating with a ship and a longboat, the Spaniards Manuel Quimper, Juan Carrasco, and Gonzalo López de Haro explored much of the coast of the Juan de Fuca Strait. In the process, Carrasco, using the longboat, reconnoitred Port Discovery and charted it.

Prior to its voyage of exploration, most of the members of the Eliza expedition had resided at Nootka for about a year, and at least some of them had learned something of the local language. The expedition's ship *San Carlos* was in Port Discovery from June 22 to July 25, 1791; so were Eliza, Pantoja, and Carrasco. Possibly, nay very likely, the storekeeper González was there as well. The schooner *Santa Saturnina* and the longboat were there between June 22 and July 1. Pantoja's report states that there was no Native habitation in the vicinity, but from time-to-time some Indians "from outside," that is, from somewhere else, went there "to barter boys."[112]

The Vancouver expedition included a few men who had in past years spent some time at Nootka, and had probably picked up a few words of the local language. The expedition carried at least one list, probably more, of words and expressions of that language and their equivalents in English. Between May 2 and May 18, 1792, the expedition was at Port Discovery. The anonymous journal attributed to Edward Bell states that,

> ...there were no habitants in it but now and then, some very quiet and inoffensive Indians went there, with two or three canoes, and engaged in barter with the expeditionaries. They were evidently a tribe that visited the Sea Coast but seldom, as they were generally clad in the skins of Land animals, and during our stay here, they brough [brought] but only one Sea Otter skin to sell...[113]

Vancouver's book says:

> A few natives in two or three canoes favored us with their company...some kind of them understood a few words of the Nootkan language...they offered for sale two children, each about six or seven years of age, and, being shown some copper, were very anxious that the bargain be closed. This, however, I peremptorily prohibited, expressing, as well as I was able, our great abhorrence of such traffic.[114]

These and other documents from the Vancouver expedition agree fairly well with Pantoja's statement to the effect that while the Eliza expedition was at Port Discovery there were no inhabitants, but that it was occasionally visited by Natives who wished to sell boys.

In some parts of the territories of what are now Washington State and the province of British Columbia, there were, without doubt, inhabitants who had

---

[112] Pantoja's report has a few details about Puerto de Quadra, i.e., Port Discovery, and adds *"sin haver Rancheria alguna en el distrito del Puerto y solo benian de fuera algunos Indios en sus Canoas de tiempo en tiempo a Cambalachear Muchachos."*

[113] Quoted in the book, *Vancouver's discovery of Puget Sound*, Edmond S. Meany, ed., 1957, p.7.

[114] Vancouver's book, Lamb 1984 edition, p.517.

domesticated horses, while inhabitants of the coastal regions were adept at travelling by canoe over long distances.

The story suggests that the people with horses dwelt on flat lands situated to the north of the boy's home, but does not add details. While there is some flat land around Puget Sound, and in the Fraser Valley, it is difficult to think of any coastal area that obviously resembles the "prairie-like" image that the boy's statement conjures up. Most of the now-agricultural land and valley bottoms of the coastal region would have been very heavily forested at the time. Any extensive grassland would have had to have been away somewhere in the interior. There is ample proof that Native people of the area had at least indirect contact with fellow Americans far away. News of European ships visiting the coast travelled very rapidly, as did trade goods and the smallpox disease.

CONJECTURE

In the light of the aforementioned facts and circumstances, I venture the following conjecture:

The boy spoke some Nuu-chah-nulth (Nootkan), or some related dialect such as Nitinat or Makah (the local language at Neah Bay), and could communicate directly with some of the Spaniards; or, if this was not the case, one of the other Native children could translate from whatever the boy's mother tongue was (a Coast Salish dialect or Chemakum) to Nuu-chah-nulth.

The boy's family, or community, dwelt somewhere on the eastern coast of Puget Sound, the region of the present-day cities and towns of Seattle, Snohomish, Everett, and Arlington.

They were eager to obtain copper sheets.

They had good canoes, were expert at navigating them, and could cover fairly long distances. They knew Discovery Bay, which they could easily reach by canoe.

Over the years, through intertribal contact, they learned about the occasional appearance of ships along the western coast of Vancouver Island, and about the Native children traded to personnel of some of these vessels. Perhaps trading children was a normal transaction for these people.

These people heard of the presence of a ship in the Juan de Fuca Strait, and of Carrasco's visit to Port Discovery, in 1790. The following year, in the course of thirty-three days (between June 29 and July 25, 1792), these people heard of the presence of the ship *San Carlos* at this anchorage. Some of these people came by canoe to the bay, and traded some children to the ship's personnel, in exchange for copper sheets. The dealings with the Spaniards was facilitated by the fact that Carrasco had already been there the previous year, so they had some idea what to expect.

One of these children was a very bright boy whom the Spaniards assumed to be eleven or twelve years old. He had seen parties of Indians coming to his home district to trade for fish. These people must clearly have come from somewhere where salmon were not readily available. These visitors were fairly different from his own kin, were accompanied by horses, and he understood that they came from some flat lands at a long distance to the north, or northeast.

With words of his language, helped by mimicry and gestures, the boy told the Spaniards something about those people and their horses. The Spaniards who had a smattering of the Nootkan language were able to understand the gist of the story, and Juan Pantoja wrote it down in his report.

To sum up, this story, though far too vague, seems basically true and provides the earliest documented evidence of visits to the Pacific Northwest Coast.

*****

In Pantoja's report, the boy's story occurs immediately after reports of the excursion of Narváez and Verdía along the eastern coast of the Strait of Georgia. This may be why a few publications of recent times assume that the boy belonged to the linguistic group called Coast Salish, and that he was acquired by Narváez in the vicinity of the present-day city of Vancouver. One of these publications states the following about Narváez:

> Certainly he talked to the Indians there. The Salish, probably from Musqueam Village, told him there was flat land for many miles up the course of the river and at the head of the valley were passes through which came strangers (the Interior Salish) to fish and stay for two moons, bringing with them goods to trade on 'large quadrupeds with round hooves and long tails and manes'.

These various assertions and assumptions have <u>no</u> basis in the records of the Eliza expedition, or in any other known documentation of the time.

Appendix 6

McMILLAN EXPEDITION OF 1824

Following Simon Fraser's visit to the Vancouver area in 1808, there is no record of any further visits by foreigners, European or American, until 1824. In November of that year, a party of forty under the leadership of James McMillan, set out from Fort George at the mouth of the Columbia River to explore the lower reaches of the Fraser River. It was the McMillan expedition that added the south (main) arm of the Fraser to the maps of the Hudson's Bay Company. As a direct result of their exploration, Fort Langley was established in 1827, and the transformation of the lower mainland area was underway.

The expedition made its way by portage and canoeing to Gray's Harbor, thence up the Chehalis River across to Puget Sound near the present-day city of Olympia. They then canoed up the east coast until, on December 11, 1824, they reached Semiahmoo Bay.

The following are a few extracts from the journal of one of the clerks of the expedition, John Work (or Wark as he more properly, but less often, is known), which describe the Greater Vancouver area at a time when it was still unvisited by foreigners other than those discussed in the main body of this work. Quotes appearing in earlier footnotes are not repeated here.

December 11–12: Semiahmoo Bay, near Birch Point: "...the shore (is) high and steep but instead of rocks are composed of clay and wooded to the water's edge, and the woods seem not to be much chocked up with underwood.... The great number of tracks seen by the hunters indicated that elk are very numerous about this place."

<u>December 13:</u> Boundary Bay: "The point above mentioned [Point Roberts] to which it was intended to cross in the morning is represented by the Indians to form the entrance of the Coweechan River[115] (which is supposed to be the same with Fraser's), on the southeast side it projects far out to sea and appears like an island but seems to be joined to the mainland which is very low by a sandy ridge which probably may be covered at high water, immense flocks of plover[116] were observed flying about the sand.... Sand appears at a distance beyond the point.... The appearance of the country round the bay from which we started this morning [Semiahmoo] round to the point [Roberts], appears low and flat, the bay appears to be shallow."

<u>December 13:</u> Nicomekl River: "In the river nothing but thick willows are seen for some distance from the water, where the banks though low are well wooded with pine, cedar, alder and some other trees. There are the appearance of beaver being pretty numerous in this river."

<u>December 14:</u> Headwaters of the Nicomekl (near Langley): "(The) portage which is to another little river [Salmon River] which falls into Coweechin River [Fraser River], lies through a plain which with the weighty rain is become so soft and miry, that in several places it resembles a swamp.... The soil here appears to be very rich, is a black mould, the remains of a luxurious crop of fern and grass lies on the ground. The country about here seems low, the trees of different kinds, pine, birch, poplar, alder, etc., some of the pine of a very large size.... Elk have been very numerous here...."

---

[115] This is the earliest known reference to the Cowichan people of Vancouver Island who evidently frequented the Fraser River in such numbers that Work's Native guides knew the river by their name.

[116] Theed Pearse in his book "Birds of the Early Explorers in the Northern Pacific" suggests these might have been Pacific Golden Plovers (*Pluvialis dominica fulva*).

December 15: Between the Nicomekl and Salmon Rivers: "The Indians came to us in the afternoon. They are of the Cahoutetts Nation.[117] They differ little in appearance from the Indians who accompany us, their blankets are of their own manufacture and made of hair or coarse wool on which they wear a kind of short cloak made of the bark of the cedar tree, it has a hole in the middle through which the head passes, it extends to below the shoulders and breast and has an opening left on each side to leave the arms unconfined. The only arms [weapons] observed with these were bows and arrows. Their language differs from that of our Indians but they understand each other."

December 16: Site of Fort Langley: "We entered the Coweechin River at 1 o'clock. At this place it is a fine looking river at least as wide as the Columbia at Oak Point, 1000 yards wide [0.9 km]...(both shores are) well wooded to the water's edge. The trees are pine, cedar, alder, birch and some others. Some high hills appear to the Eastward at no great distance, topped with snow. From the size and appearance of the river there is no doubt in our minds that it is Fraser's."

December 17: Site of Fort Langley to Hatzic (*Xat'suq'*) Slough: "In the forepart of the day we saw an Indian lodge in a little bay on the north side of the river.... This was a miserable habitation formed of plank, both sides and roof, the usual appendages of Indian houses filth and nastiness were here in abundance, and the smell of the remains of decayed salmon was very offensive. In number 22, 7 men, 7 women and 8 children. Nevertheless, the inhabitants appeared healthy and seemed to have plenty of dried salmon provided.... We learned that they got some fine European articles in traffic from tribes above whom obtained them from White people."

December 18: Upriver from Hatzic: "About 9 o'clock 47 men, 3 women, and 1 boy of the Cahantitt Indians [Kwantlen]...visited us in a friendly manner.... A good deal of information was received from these people respecting the river. A little boy presented to the chief to forward to

---

[117] Undoubtedly a member of the Stó:lō Nation. The Kwantlen moved to the area of Fort Langley after it was established. The name Kwantlen is particularly difficult for non-Indians; the "Handbook of North American Indians," Volume 7, lists as synonyms Cahantitt, Cahotitt, Cahoutetts, Kʻoāʼantel, Quaitlin, Quāltl, Quatline, Quitline, and Quoitland.

Thompson's River, he mentioned not fewer than 15 tribes, 8 on the south and 7 on the north side of the river, through whose hands it must pass before it reached the Forks. He named the Suswhaps [Shuswap Nation of the Cariboo area] and some other tribes whose names we know.... They wore mats to keep off the rain and conical hats. On account of our short stay we could observe nothing respecting their manners or mode of living of these people. They offered some roasted sturgeon for sale...but of their mode of taking them we know nothing. Our Indian guide understood them and was understood also. The language they speak has some little resemblance to the Okanagan."

Work is unclear as to how far upstream of present-day Mission the party travelled, but it was evidently not far as after what seems to have been a fair amount of socializing with the Native people, they turned back about noon and returned to the camp at Hatzic Slough.

December 19: Down river to Lulu Island: "During the day the river maintained its wideness till towards evening when its breadth considerably increased.... Where we are now encamped is not far from the entrance of the river, the country is so very swampy and liable to be overflowed with the tide that we had to turn back some distance to our present situation which, though the site of an old village, is a quagmire.... Though we saw but very few Indians yet they must be very numerous about this river at particular seasons of the year. We passed the site of several old villages, the one where we are now encamped [Lulu Island, opposite Tilbury Island?] extends at least 3/4 of a mile along the shore [1.2 km], while passing it I counted 54 houses but on coming near they are found to be so situated that not more than the 1/2 of them were counted.... Four canoes containing 17 Indians of the Cahotitt tribe [Kwantlen] met us...and seemed highly pleased (at the motive for our visit). The old chief seems to be marked with smallpox, and is a smart-looking man though pretty old."

December 20: To the sea: "Saw a canoe with six Indians near the entrance of the River.... These people are of the Coweechin tribe and had just crossed from Vancouver's Island where they now live. They did not approach near enough for us to distinguish anything of their dress or appearance, they were armed with long spears. On the low land at the entrance of the River geese, particularly white ones,[118] were very numerous and were no means shy, they allowed us to approach easily."

The expedition rounded Point Roberts and camped in Vancouver's Birch Bay on December 20, and made their way back to Fort George, arriving on December 30, 1824. During their visit to the Vancouver area, they had experienced showers, rain, or "weighty" rain on almost every day.

When McMillan returned to the area to establish Fort Langley, he came in the schooner *Cadboro* which was the first ship of any size to enter the Fraser. Several unsuccessful attempts were initially made to enter the river, and the ship dragged anchor and drifted out to sea over night. Shortly after, the ship grounded, but was not damaged. They eventually found deep water and reached the site of the fort on July 29, 1827.

---

[118] Snow Geese (*Chen hyperborea*). They still winter in large numbers in the Fraser estuary.

INDEX